A HISTORY OF LIBRARIES IN GREAT BRITAIN AND NORTH AMERICA

A
HISTORY OF LIBRARIES
IN GREAT BRITAIN
AND
NORTH AMERICA

BY

Albert Predeek

TRANSLATED BY

Lawrence S. Thompson

AMERICAN LIBRARY ASSOCIATION

CHICAGO, 1947

Manufactured in the United States of America

TRANSLATOR'S PREFACE

There is relatively little in the first two volumes of the great Milkau-Leyh *Handbuch der Bibliothekswissenschaft* which does not have a counterpart in the Anglo-American literature of historical bibliography and library administration. But the third volume, a monumental history of libraries in over a thousand pages, represents a field which has not been systematically treated in English since the publication of Edward Edwards' *Memoirs*. E. A. Savage, J. W. Clark, and James W. Thompson have made important contributions to medieval library history; but the modern period, and particularly the last century, has received only sporadic attention in English-speaking countries.

The first and only study of British and American libraries from the Renaissance to the beginning of World War II has been contributed to the third volume of the *Handbuch* by Dr. Albert Predeek, director of the library of the Technische Hochschule in Berlin-Charlottenburg, which was bombed and burned in November 1943. Dr. Predeek has travelled widely in both countries and enjoyed the personal friendship of outstanding librarians. While in America, he spent three months making a detailed study of the organization and administration of a leading midwestern land-grant college library. In addition to this firsthand experience, he has read widely in the literature of Anglo-American librarianship and has written several important monographs and articles on the subject, some of which have been translated into English.

While the present work will be welcomed by librarians and historians alike, it does not pretend to be the final word on the subject. Indeed, the effects of World War II on libraries all over the world will necessitate not only the reorganization of library policy but also the rewriting of library history. But Dr. Predeek has supplied us with the necessary apparatus without which any new essay in the field would be inordinately difficult. For the present this monograph will have to serve as a very adequate stopgap.

Seven years have elapsed between the publication of the original and the completion of this translation. Since that time the final chapter has been written in the history of many historic British libraries, the national policy of American librarianship has been revised to meet the impact of the times, and important articles and books on library history have been published.* The processes of scholarship are too slow to keep pace with the processes of twentieth-century history; but the product of this scholarship, however tardy, will be an invaluable aid to future generations in their attempt to avoid the errors of the past.

A few changes have been made by the translator in the text and notes without the knowledge of the author because of the extreme difficulty of communications at this time.

The translator is deeply grateful to Dr. Predeek and to Mr. Otto Harrassowitz, the German publisher, for their generosity in granting permission to publish an English translation. The execution and successful completion of the translation is due in large measure to the vigorous interest of Dr. Charles H. Brown. In addition, there is a special obligation to Dr. Harry Miller Lydenberg, friend of all bookmen, who managed to establish contact between the translator and the author at a time when communications were otherwise impossible.

LAWRENCE S. THOMPSON
Kalamazoo, Michigan
January 1947

* No attempt has been made to expand or to bring up to date the bibliography in the original text.

CONTENTS

I. GREAT BRITAIN FROM 1500 TO THE PRESENT

Contents

II. THE UNITED STATES OF AMERICA

Contents

Part I

GREAT BRITAIN FROM 1500 TO THE PRESENT

INTRODUCTION[1]

In the Middle Ages English libraries were still a part of the general European cultural scene, but in modern times they have gone their own way in accordance with the peculiarities of Anglo-Saxon institutional development. There were few contacts with Continental libraries, and these were of little importance until fairly recently. Along with English imperialism, books and libraries also found their way to America, where, under new conditions, an Anglo-Saxon library tradition developed which ultimately had a fruitful influence on the mother country. Likewise, the European continent felt American influences; but they came by a direct route and, in turn, directed the attention of European librarians to developments in modern English libraries. Certainly the British Museum of the nineteenth century and the brilliant work of Panizzi did not fail to impress the European and German library world; and librarians and scholars of all lands made the pilgrimage to this mecca of books or to the ancient seats of English learning. Nevertheless, awareness of English librarianship as such first appeared on the German horizon towards the end of the century. The organization, the methods of administration, and even some librarians must have seemed unusual to the German observer; but it must not be forgotten that methods of instruction and research and the arts and sciences have developed in Great Britain under conditions quite distinct from Continental Europe and Germany in particular. No English king has been a godfather to the universities, libraries, and scientific institutions; and similarly the regulatory, patronizing, and guiding hand of the state has been absent almost up until the present day. The majority of all cultural institutions owe their conception and development to private corporate initiative or to the generosity of wealthy gentlemen.

Introduction

Of course, the wealth of the British Empire with its worldwide ramifications was behind all these phenomena. English merchants, soldiers, diplomats, collectors, and travellers have carried the political ideas and power politics of their nation into the most distant lands; but, in some measure of exchange, they have also brought back to their island kingdom the intellectual, scientific, and artistic wealth of all times and all nations. Whatever England has incorporated into her archives, libraries, and museums during the nineteenth century, which was so decisive for the expansion and power of the British Empire, has become not merely a treasure of the nation but also of mankind. After a long period of insular isolationism British librarians have fully recognized in recent years the duties incumbent upon them as guardians of these treasures, and they have made significant contributions of value not only to themselves but also to librarianship in general.

CHAPTER ONE

FROM THE REFORMATION TO THE END OF THE SEVENTEENTH CENTURY

THE DESTRUCTION OF THE OLDER LIBRARIES[2]

The English Reformation was partially a religious and partially a political movement. Declaration of absolute royal authority over the property of churches, abbeys, and cloisters followed the investiture of Henry VIII as head of the Anglican Church in 1534. To be sure, the Acts of Dissolution of 1535 and 1539[3] attempted to justify the transfer of church property to the crown as a voluntary move, but their execution revealed the true purposes. Royal commissioners, in many instances shady characters, were provided with unlimited authority, and they instituted sham investigations of the conditions in abbeys and cloisters. Denouncers and slanderers were easily found, and economic or moral abuses gave a basis or an excuse for dissolution and expropriation of wealth. From the smaller cloisters alone Henry is alleged to have received an annual income of £30,000.[4]

Plundering and destruction followed the dissolutions. The famous Abbey of Hyde in Winchester, a foundation of Alfred the Great as well as his burial place, was laid in ruins; and the best part of the library was given to the Chancellor of the Exchequer, Thomas Cromwell, while the remainder was scattered and destroyed. From the rich library of the Cloister of Glastonbury, legendary grave of King Arthur, only a few manuscripts were saved. St. Albans, seat of a famous scriptorium and school of painting, was ruined. Whole libraries were sold for a few shillings to shopkeepers and bookbinders without regard for the content; and whole boatloads of books are alleged to have been shipped to the Continent, much to the astonishment of other nations.[5] If Henry ever had an idea of increasing his own library with a part of the booty, he soon gave it up. It seemed more important to him to win support for his claims to supremacy and for his divorces through gestures of royal favor and gifts to high prelates and noblemen. This is the reason why the cathedral libraries were scarcely touched by the plunderings and why they could hold to their property until the seventeenth century, when they lost a part of it in the iconoclasm of the civil war.[6]

In addition to the cathedral churches, various colleges also received grants, but under Edward VI they too suffered from the forces of destruction. Fanatical commissioners of the Reformation "purged" the libraries of Oxford and Cambridge of missals, lives of saints, and "superstitious" tracts. The Publick Library of Cambridge saved only nineteen manuscripts out of 330, the Publick Library of Oxford only three or four out of 600, while individual colleges could display their catalogues as plaintive witnesses of losses suffered. "Thus fell the famous old English monasteries," writes Edwards,[7] but, he adds, "True Captains of men lived and died there, who after many a hard struggle won enduring victories against brutish violence, emasculating ignorance, and decorous mammon-worship." Among them a place of honor belongs to John Leland,[8] the learned collector and student of early English history and language. As Royal Antiquary he travelled through England from 1536 to 1543, too late to stop the plundering but early enough to prevent the complete destruction of the libraries. In all probability the losses have been exaggerated by contemporaries as well as posterity. A large proportion of the works from dissolved cloisters and those subjected to official inspection has been preserved in the libraries of colleges, cathedrals, and the great private collectors. Princes of the church like Archbishops Parker and Ussher, bibliophiles like Sir Robert Cotton, Sir Thomas Bodley, John Dee, Baron Lumley and others, could still preserve considerable portions of old collections for the nation in the latter part of the sixteenth century and entire seventeenth century.

THE LIBRARIES OF THE UNIVERSITIES[9]

In the stormy years between Henry VIII and Elizabeth the colleges, like the cloisters and the churches, were exposed to every attack by the masters of the state. Their library catalogues reveal not only acquisition and loss of books but also the ebb and flow of scholarship. Leland's inventories of libraries which remained intact reveal a marked similarity in collections all over England. Above all, biblical, scholastic and philosophical tracts, and Latin classics are represented. Greek and humanistic authors and the occasional mathematical, medical, and scientific works are less numerous.[10] In Oxford and Cambridge, however, books on art and architecture and even the Arabic authors stood in high repute. Erasmus had sojourned in Oxford from 1498 to 1499 and in Cambridge from 1511 to 1514 as a forerunner of Greek studies, humanism, and the Reformation. When Leland visited Oxford, he found a long list of humanistic authors, among them Salutati and Aretino. But Luther's writings were burned in 1521 in London and at both universities on the orders of Cardinal Wolsey. Upon Wolsey's downfall in 1535 the unfriendly attitude toward the Reformation was reversed; and with the burning of Duns Scotus' writings at New College, Oxford, scholasticism was buried in England.[11]

The colleges and universities were sadly disappointed if they had expected to gain much from the dissolution of the cloisters; but on the whole the days of Henry VIII and Wolsey were not bad for their libraries.[12] Wolsey, Chancellor of Oxford from 1518 on, founded Christ Church and its library, for whose expansion he made great plans. John Fisher, Chancellor of Cambridge and the learned friend of Erasmus and the humanists, favored especially the libraries of Queen's College and Christ's College. Both universities were also spared from violence during Thomas Cromwell's chancellorship; but after his downfall in 1540 persecutions and suppression of the religious houses and the colleges began. After Henry's death it became even more intense. At that time the student enrollment in Oxford and Cambridge fell to less than half. In 1550 the Reformation Commission attacked the Publick Library in Oxford, the promising foundation of Duke Humphrey of Gloucester, destroyed almost all manuscripts of "popish" content, sold the remainder to bookbinders and tailors, and removed the furnishings.[13] When the Cambridge University Library was inspected in 1538 it had to give up all "offensive" books; and in 1550 it contained only 180 volumes, fewer than it had owned a hundred years earlier.[14]

7

The short period of counter-reformation under Mary brought new inspections but no new losses. The accession of Elizabeth to the throne signalled a long period of rest for the universities and of growth for the libraries. Although the Acts of Supremacy, the Acts of Uniformity, and the oath on the Thirty-nine Articles made the universities creatures of the Anglican Church, from that time on not merely clergymen but also laymen, future officials, jurists, physicians, and "gentlemen," pursued the learned studies. The curriculum was changed, and with it the contents of the libraries. Nevertheless, the intellectual and material progress of the Elizabethan Age benefited the university libraries less than those of the colleges, for the latter enjoyed a much more influential position than the former.

THE SEVENTEENTH CENTURY

In 1587 Sir Thomas Bodley decided to give up his diplomatic career and "to set up his Staffe at the Librarie dore in Oxon."[15] Considerable wealth acquired by a rich marriage enabled him to repair the old library of Duke Humphrey; and it was reopened in 1602 with 2,000 volumes in the rooms of the Old Library, which are still in use at the present time. Bodley's solicitude for his foundation was comprehensive and farsighted. He not only endowed it with gifts of land and a legacy of £7000 but also was able to secure gifts of books or money from numerous influential friends. He engaged in the actual business of the library with exact policies. He decided which books were to be reinstated and thereby revealed his humanistic bent. English ephemera and light reading were rejected as trash, translations from Latin and Greek banned,[16] and first editions, like the Shakespeare folio of 1623, were considered superfluous upon the appearance of a new edition.[17] The agreement made in 1610 with the London Stationers' Company by which the latter consented to present a perfect copy of every book "printed in the said Companue of Stationers" was most significant.[18] Bodley lived to see the completion of the first annex in 1613. When the first librarian, Thomas James, retired from office in 1620, the library contained 16,000 volumes.

In view of the uncertainty of the times many important private collections found refuge in the library. The Barocci collection of

242 volumes of Greek manuscripts owned by the Earl of Pembroke, was acquired in 1629, and in 1634 the collection of 238 volumes of English historical manuscripts owned by Sir Kenelm Digby. In addition, the library added 1,300 manuscript volumes in twenty languages from the collection of Archbishop Laud in 1635-46; and the most significant acquisition of the seventeenth century was the 8,000 volume collection of Greek and oriental manuscripts presented by the lawyer John Selden and housed according to his will in the west annex, "Selden's End" (1640).[19] Fortunately the Bodleian, as it was known after 1649, was spared in the civil wars. In the age of the Stuarts and the Commonwealth it assumed first rank among the libraries of the land. James I said that the founder deserved the name "Sir Thomas Godley,"[20] and posterity has honored Bodley no less. The title of office, Bodley's Librarian, perpetuates forever the name of the man who created the first functional library of modern times.

The Cambridge University Library[21] was not favored with the good fortune of her sister in Oxford. After promising beginnings in the second half of the sixteenth century when it received rich donations of books and manuscripts from the Archbishop of Canterbury, Matthew Parker,[22] it entered into a period of dormancy in the seventeenth century. In part prospective gifts were prevented by cramped quarters. This circumstance was felt as early as 1586, and by 1610 it had become so serious as to prevent the removal of the magnificent library of Archbishop Bancroft of Canterbury to Cambridge. Plans for a new building[23] were often close to realization but had to be put aside for more than a hundred years following the outbreak of the civil wars. Acquisitions during the seventeenth century were scanty. In 1632 the library received a valuable collection of Arabic manuscripts from the library of Thomas Erpenius of Leyden. In 1647 the Parliament of the Commonwealth granted £500 for the purchase of the Isaac Pragi collection of Hebrew manuscripts, and in 1648 it granted £2000 for requisitioning the Bancroft Library, which, however, had to be returned to the Archiepiscopal Library at Lambeth after the Restoration.[24]

The university and the colleges suffered badly during the civil wars from occupations, levies and sequestrations; and on top of this came ordinances for the removal of all "superstitious" objects in the churches and libraries. Of course, individual college libraries, for example, Peterhouse and St. Johns, were enriched by book collections and property taken from royalists or those who refused to take the Oath of the Covenant.[25] The political and intellectual strife of the seventeenth century gradually brought books from private ownership back into circulation, and frequently they went into the libraries of the universities, for which gifts and endowments had become almost the only means of increasing holdings. Around the turn of the seventeenth century there were almost 25,000 volumes in the Bodleian, but the number in the Cambridge University Library fell far below this figure. All told the Oxford libraries could claim 7,000 manuscripts at that time, almost half of the total number in England.

The Scottish universities and their libraries are younger than the English.[26] St. Andrews (1411) was sacrificed to the Reformation, and during the sixteenth century and up to 1634 Aberdeen was scarcely mentioned. The University of Glasgow Library, founded simultaneously with the university in 1453, survived the crisis of the Reformation. With the founding of the Scottish Presbyterian Church by John Knox in 1560 a profound change took place. During his years of exile the reformer had the opportunity of becoming acquainted with the cultures of France, Germany, and Switzerland, and he had worked with Calvin in Geneva and Bullinger in Zürich. He revealed a deep understanding for schools and libraries, and from that time on their development went forward under the dominant influences of Presbyterianism. In 1582 the fourth Scottish university was founded in Edinburgh, and its library attained some significance in the first third and toward the end of the seventeenth century. However, the University of Glasgow, which had received important endowments repeatedly since 1630, assumed a leading position.

In Ireland[27] scholarly libraries originated in the seventeenth century. The beginning of the first, the library of Trinity College in Dublin, is noteworthy. The English army in Munster, victorious over the Spaniards and Irish insurgents in the Battle of Kinsale (Christmas Eve of 1601), turned over a collection of £1,800 (£700 in the *Book of Benefactors*) to the college for the purchase of books as "a memorial of the gallantry of military men, and of that due respect which they had for true religion and learning." James Ussher,[28] afterwards primate, was entrusted with these funds and sent to England to make purchases, where he enjoyed scholarly as well as social contacts with Bodley, Camden, Selden, Laud, and other collectors. As early as 1604 the Trinity College Library, which had been opened with forty books, possessed over 4,000 volumes. In addition Ussher's valuable private collection of 10,000 volumes had been willed to the college; but after varying fortunes it fell in danger of being sold outside the country. Again the military, this time Cromwell's army, intervened and gathered funds to save the collection. Finally the 7,094 volumes and 603 selected manuscripts were handed over to the Irish House of Commons in 1661 and in turn given to the college.

PRIVATE COLLECTIONS[29]

In the sixteenth and seventeenth centuries there were no libraries owned by the community and supported by public appropriation. On the contrary all libraries were the property of corporations or of private individuals. According to Renaissance ideas, a collection of books was a mark of wealth; humanism and the Reformation viewed the book as a means of education and a document of the past; and in the political and religious struggles of the sixteenth century the book and the broadside were weapons. Hardly any library survived its founder, for the heir viewed it only as a piece of property; and only the learned bibliophile would give his collection to his college, his church, or his professional association. The destruction of the cloister libraries aroused curiosity about their remnants. When the travels and studies of antiquarians on the Continent attracted notice to foreign literatures and interest in natural sciences increased during the latter half of the seventeenth century, these categories of books found their way into private libraries. During the civil wars collections of a political character appeared for the first time. Belleslettres appeared in more refined libraries at a relatively late date. Even slower than the cavalier poets in working their way into the libraries were the literary standard bearers of the intellectual movements, Milton's pathos and Bunyan's ethos.

11

As late as Milton's day reading and learning had no place in a general education; but in 1622 Henry Peacham's *Compleat Gentleman* had at least required the possession of a library in handsome format. The external appearance of a collection of books, particularly the binding, meant more than content; and it was only in the latter part of the seventeenth century that auctions and book lists carried the knowledge of books to broader circles. In addition, noblemen, gentlemen scholars, and prosperous burghers also appeared on the scene as connoisseurs and collectors. The English kings were not enthusiastic collectors. To be sure, Henry VII had brought together a choice collection of Vérard imprints;[30] but to the hedonistic Henry VIII books and manuscripts meant little more than salable wares, and Leland gives no especial recognition to the fact that he enriched the royal library with more than a hundred manuscripts.[31]

Elizabeth loved costly books, but she also loved money; and in 1598 the German traveller Paul Hentzner found her library "well stored with Greek, Latin, Italian, and French books. . . . All these books are bound in velvet of different colours, though mostly red with clasps of gold and silver; some base pearls and precious stones set in their bindings."[32] But Elizabeth hardly enjoyed an intimate acquaintance with her library; and this was probably also the reason for the failure of a projected Elizabethan Academy, for which Sir Humphrey Gilbert had submitted a detailed and reasoned proposal in 1570, with a library to be based on legal deposit and steady revenue.[33] Archbishop Parker's movement to create a kind of national library from the royal library was also unsuccessful. At all events, Roger Ascham, the librarian of Mary and Elizabeth, was able to acquire several collections of historical documents as well as the manuscripts from Martin Butzer's collection. The first real connoisseur and collector was Prince Henry, son of James I, who died young in 1612, but to whom we are indebted for the purchase of highly important manuscripts from the collections of the Earl of Arundel, Archbishop Cranmer, and the dissolved cloisters.[34] Charles I was perhaps the only ruler who understood the value of a library. However Charles II was also agreeably disposed to increasing the collections of St. James. During his reign the old Royal Library received depository rights by the Licensing Act of 1662,[35] and the number of volumes rose to 10,000. When Richard Bentley took office as librarian in 1694, the Royal Library had already become semipublic.

What the Tudors and Stuarts had done half-heartedly was the second nature of the high prelates, for almost all of them were book collectors. The spirit of scholasticism, combined with humanistic learning, still lived in their hearts; and many of them withdrew from religious and political struggle voluntarily or involuntarily to spend their time among books and manuscripts. Richard de Bury found more than one imitator. One of the earliest patrons of Cambridge was Thomas Scot, Archbishop of York (died 1500);[36] and one of his successors, Tobias Matthew (died 1629), willed to the city of Bristol a part of his collections as the basis for a public library. Cathedral libraries, founded by endowments or legacies of bishops, were also public in the sense that they were designed for clerical use, and their perpetuation was carefully insured. Above the names of all other prelates stand those of the archbishops of Canterbury whose munificence was expressed in rich gifts not only to their own Lambeth Library[37] but also to many other libraries.

The collections of Wolsey and Cranmer were confiscated after their fall, but Matthew Parker (1504-75)[38] began a new and brilliant epoch. This prelate, without a peer as philanthropist, scholar, antiquarian, and collector, created the primary bases for orderly administration as well as scientific care of books and manuscripts. He secured permission to transfer historically important documents from private ownership to the state; and he made John Bale responsible for the safety of manuscripts which came from the cloisters.[39] Agents gathered 6,700 manuscript volumes for him in four years, and copyists were constantly provided with exact technical directions. His solicitude was especially directed at the preservation of monuments of national literature, for he had Irish manuscripts brought to England and edited Anglo-Saxon manuscripts himself. In letters to his friend Flacius Illyricus he let it be understood that he could not permit German agents to comb England for old documents.[40] He ordered that all new books be brought to his attention, not simply for reasons of ecclesiastical discipline, but also to become acquainted with the new offerings of English and German publishers. Unlike Bodley, Parker did not found a great functional library, but he presented his treasures generously to existing libraries, patronizing the libraries of Corpus Christi, Caius, Trinity, and the Cambridge University Library in particular. Thus relatively little remained for the Lambeth Library, and his successor, Richard Bancroft,[41] was the first to will his private library to the episcopal see.

The last great collector of Lambeth was William Sancroft (died 1693) [42] who retired in exile to Fressingfield with his rich library after his deposition in 1670. Later his library was divided between Lambeth, Emanuel College in Cambridge, and the Bodleian. In the line of the great clerical collectors of the seventeenth century belong also the Archbishop of Armagh, James Ussher, and his successor, Narcissus Marsh (died 1713). With a magnanimity like Parker's, Marsh bought books and manuscripts in England and on the Continent in order to leave them to his diocese, but in part also to the Bodleian.[43]

Under the last Tudors, and under Elizabeth in particular, laymen gradually replaced clerics in high offices of the court and state. Not only art treasures and books were concentrated in the hands of these notables but also quantities of political correspondence and state papers. Frequently their owners ended in the Tower or on the gallows; but seldom, and never systematically, were these collections safely put away for state purposes, and invaluable treasures were lost or had to be bought again at great cost for state collections. Thus the comprehensive political correspondence of Robert Devereux, Elizabeth's favorite and Bacon's friend, fell into the hands of his enemy, Robert Cecil, whose own papers went in part to Sir Robert Cotton, in part to the historian John Strype, and ultimately to the British Museum.[44] Likewise the large collections of other great statesmen at the court of Queen Elizabeth, for example, Sir Walter Raleigh, the Lord Chancellor Sir Nicholas Bacon (died 1579), and his great son, Sir Francis, were scattered broadcast in the course of long peregrinations. In those uncertain times rise and fall came close together, and seldom did a great library survive the generation of its founder.

After Elizabeth, English affairs spread further and further away from the Island Kingdom. Ambassadors, statesmen, scholars, and merchants undertook long journeys and brought home valuable collections. One of the most important libraries of the time was acquired by the widely travelled connoisseur of books and fine arts, Thomas Howard, Earl of Arundel (died 1646).[45] After 1628 it was shelved with princely taste in the Arundel House, a forerunner of the British Museum, and made accessible to friends and scholars. Here, in addition to the Arundel marbles and other museum pieces, was also the famous library of Willibald Pirckheimer. In 1666 the grandson of the founder, Henry Howard, presented the books, manuscripts and letters to the Royal Society, from which they were passed on to the British Museum in 1831-32 by way of exchange.

The last decades of the seventeenth century witnessed the foundation of many new libraries since political and economic conditions had become somewhat steadier. During this period some great family libraries which have been preserved to the present day were founded. Among them was the Biblioteca Lindesiana, founded by the earls of Balcarres[46] and their heirs, a library which we shall meet again in one of the great municipal libraries.[47] At the same time the dukes of Marlborough founded their library at Blenheim, a collection which numbered 17,000 volumes by the beginning of the nineteenth century.

Half of the hundred private libraries formed in the course of the seventeenth century were owned by lawyers, scholars, and middle-class collectors.[48] By the beginning of the eighteenth century this proportion had increased even more in favor of learned connoisseurs and users of books, to whom the book was something more than a valuable or a rarity. Thus an inner change in libraries may be observed. Practical purposes came to the forefront, and the owner made his collection accessible to friends, students, and scholars. In one sense these libraries, which contained the choice literature of all fields, were the forerunners of public libraries. The names Camden, Cotton, and Selden[49] shone like a triple star in the literary heaven of the age. The historian William Camden (died 1623) and the lawyer John Selden (died 1654) owned extremely valuable collections. Camden's library passed to his friend Robert Cotton (died 1631), and Selden's collection of more than 8,000 volumes went mainly to the Bodleian *(supra)*.

But the foundation stone of all scholarly work at that time was the immensely rich collection of Cotton,[50] which was open to all comers in the London home of the owner. Here Bodley and Ussher met. Here one might have met the alchemist, spiritualist, and friend of Mercator, John Dee, who failed to find the alkahest, to be sure, but did uncover extremely valuable astronomical and alchemistic books and manuscripts. Here Henry Savile, John Speed, Francis Bacon, and Camden studied and wrote historical works; and as late as the eighteenth century John Strype used the collection for his historical biographies and Thomas Rymer for his *Foedera*. The library of the Cotton House covered all periods of English history, and its state papers, documents, and records enjoyed official authority. Indeed, the valuable collection was Cotton's ill fortune, since it was repeatedly misused for political or personal feuds. Cotton himself got into difficulties with influential men, and during the reign of Charles I his house was known as the central point of the opposition. After numerous measures directed against the owner, the library was seized and released only after his death. Cotton's son, Sir Thomas, tided it over the civil wars. His son, Sir John (1621-1701), the third baronet, intended to leave it to the nation, but it was rather Sir John's grandson, also named John (1679-1731), who carried out this purpose. By an act of Parliament in 1700 the Cotton Library was incorporated into the property of the state and in 1753 transferred to the British Museum.[51]

The libraries of professional corporations, in particular the flourishing legal libraries of seventeenth-century London, may be classed as private libraries only in a few respects. To be sure, they were restricted in use to members, but actually they were open to the general public. The oldest London legal corporation, Lincoln's Inn, established a library as early as 1508,[52] but it first attained significance after one of the most famous members, Sir Matthew Hale (died 1776), willed it his collections of legal documents and correspondence gathered over a period of forty years. The legal antiquary William Petyt (died 1707) also presented his collection of manuscripts to the corporation of barristers in the Inner Temple on the condition that the public should have free access.[53] But the earliest and clearest manifestation of a public library was the old Guildhall Library[54] which was founded by the Lord Mayor of London, Richard Whittington (died 1423), as a "common library" for all students. It lasted only a short time, for during the Reformation it was borrowed by the Lord Protector, Edward Seymour, Duke of Somerset, and not returned. The new Guildhall Library did not celebrate its resurrection until 1828. The library founded together with Sion College[55] by Dr. Thomas White for the use of the London guild of parochial clergy originated in a private collection. After it had suffered heavily in the great London fire of 1666, it was reconstructed by subscription and granted depository rights by Queen Anne in 1709. Almost public from the very beginning was the Chetham Library[56] founded in Manchester in 1653 in connection with a hospital for the education of poor boys and named for the donor. It has enjoyed an uninterrupted existence to the present day.

LIBRARY ADMINISTRATION, CATALOGUES, AND LIBRARIANS

During this whole period a steady income was the exception. Bodley had provided his foundation with rents from capital investments and land,[57] but of the £340 to which it amounted until the end of the seventeenth century, only about £30 was available for purchases. The university granted larger appropriations for the first times in 1735 and 1750.[58] The first official appropriation for the Cambridge University Library was granted in 1648 by Parliament.[59] An endowment of £1000 given in 1666 by Bishop Tobias Rustat, Yeoman of the King's Robes, brought an annual income of £50,[60] but it was not until the eighteenth century that the university had a fixed source of income through subscriptions. On the other hand, colleges of both universities received at an early date regular gifts and endowments which laid the basis for their prosperity. Archbishop Parker showed unparalleled solicitude for St. Johns and particularly Corpus Christi (Cambridge), whose collection was described by the ecclesiastical historian Fuller as "the sun of English antiquity, but now no more than the moon, since that of Sir Robert Cotton is risen up."[61] In Scotland there seems to have been more respect for a solid basis from the very beginning. From 1653 on the Glasgow University Library derived a fixed income from a heavy endowment by the rector and vice-chancellor Zachary Boyd, and the historian Dr. Robert Johnston left the University of Edinburgh £12,000 and his collection of books in 1639.[62] Endowments of money for the library of Trinity College in Dublin have already been mentioned.[63] From fees for matriculation and graduation the universities acquired other sources of income which were gradually applied to the libraries. In Lincoln's Inn every member "called to the bench" after 1608 had to pay a fee of twenty shillings for the purchase of books. The Chetham Library was one of the few English libraries which was supported by a fixed income from the beginning.

Fortuitous incomes were reflected also in the slow growth of the collections. At the death of Thomas James in 1629 the Bodleian had 16,000 volumes, and 25,000 at the retirement of Thomas Hyde in 1701. The agreement made by Bodley with the Stationer's Company could scarcely have been a fruitful one, for in 1688 Hyde had to go to London to collect many items long overdue.[64] The Cambridge University Library showed 30,000 volumes in an obviously inexact inventory of 1751.[65] Likewise the Scottish libraries attained only modest proportions. On the other hand, the private libraries could show relatively far larger numbers. The Royal Library had about 12,000 volumes toward the middle of the seventeenth century, and the Lambeth Library contained as many as 15,000.[66] John Moore, Bishop of Ely (died 1714), owned a widely used collection of 29,000 books and 1,790 manuscripts, shelved in his London Ely House, famous throughout Europe.[67] But perhaps the most amazing collection was that of the London bookdealer George Thomason who brought together 22,255 ephemeral polemical brochures during the civil wars. Probably no other library during the entire century covered a definitely specialized field.[68] Energetic pursuit of a fixed policy of acquisition was also more customary among private collectors than among the university and college libraries, which depended chiefly on gifts.

It was an old custom for testators, donors, and founders to have their wishes and purposes defined in statutes. Even the older university library in Oxford had a statute of 1412, and Bodley's statute of 1610 remained formally in force until 1913.[69] The few effective rules for the Cambridge University Library were set forth in 1582 and 1748 by a permanent statute of the Senate which remained in force until 1849.[70] In Glasgow the first orders "concerning the biblio-theck" were drawn up in 1659 with regulations on the purchase, stamping and entering of books and on lending and fees. They were renewed by statutes of 1712 and 1715.[71] One of the most remarkable regulations was made by Samuel Pepys, who left his library to Magdalene College in Cambridge with the conditions that it remain in the unusal shelving system devised by himself, that it never be moved, and that it not be augmented by new accessions. These regulations have been scrupulously observed to the present day.[72]

The chief purpose of all these statutes was to protect books from mutilation and theft, a fact which sheds an uncomplimentary light on the habits of patrons. Richard de Bury had issued moving complaints against abuses of books; and Bodley had categorically decreed that only graduates and the founders could use the books, since other patrons, with their gaping, chattering, and continuous movement, would only cause perpetual disturbances. Almost universally the libraries forbade the lending of manuscripts and in most cases of books as well. In Oxford this rule was so strictly enforced that even Charles I and Cromwell were unable to borrow a manuscript from the Bodleian; and Selden is alleged to have been so disgruntled at a similar refusal that he withdrew the intended presentation of his library.[73] The librarian Thomas Barlow instituted the prohibition on circulation in view of the stipulated privileges for visiting scholars, but even these patrons often had to submit to onerous restrictions. The Cambridge University Library alone can claim the honor of having granted freedom of use and outside loans from the very beginning. In the private and endowed libraries abuses were the order of the day. As late as the seventeenth century Chetham prescribed chaining for all books and manuscripts in his library at Manchester, and Sir Matthew Hale did the same for the Lincoln's Inn Library.

The insecurity of the libraries is reflected by the fate of the priceless Caxtons and other books in the cathedral library at Lincoln. Its books were gradually sold or removed after 1650 to such a degree as to inspire Edwards to call this library "bibliographically famous for the books which it does not possess."[74] Sir Robert Cotton complained bitterly about losses occasioned by procrastinating and forgetful borrowers, but, like his friend Selden, he was also guilty of the same fault. But perhaps the most nonchalant borrower of other people's books was Dr. Samuel Johnson, the greatest connoisseur as well as the poorest collector. He handled borrowed books like his own, covering them with marginal annotations and seldom returning them so that after his death it was virtually impossible to determine what belonged to him and what belonged to others.[75] In general the use of public libraries was not very heavy, in part as a result of restrictions on borrowing. According to the register in the Bodleian twelve to fifteen quartos were given out daily, and no statistics were taken to show use of the chained folios.

In the sixteenth and seventeenth centuries there was neither agreement nor clear understanding concerning the nature and purpose of catalogues.[76] The catalogue was primarily an inventory with its order determined by the shelving of the books. Bibliographical entries were capricious and inexact, often incorrect. An analysis of the title page and distinction between editions according to their value was next to unknown. The science of bibliography was first applied at the book auctions in the late seventeenth century. At all events there is a significant difference between the notes on holdings taken by Leland and Hyde's catalogue of the Bodleian of 1674.

The history of English cataloguing begins in 1605 when the first printed catalogue of the Bodleian and the second one in all history appeared. It was classified according to the four faculties, arranged within these classes according to author, and had an appended author index.[77] In the second edition of 1620 James put all the titles in a single alphabet because, as he stated, of the difficulties involved in dividing the books of one author into several classes, and thereby he made a significant advance. From that time on the catalogue was no longer an inventory, and the author catalogue was clearly divorced from the shelf list. Consistency should now have required that shelf locations be added to the titles, but this step was reserved for a much later date. The third catalogue appeared in two folio volumes in 1674[78] and showed important progress. It no longer contained manuscripts, but it was complete for all printed works, even analyzing polygraphic collections. It attempted to identify the authors of anonymous works and gave cross references to them as well as to synonymous titles. The catalogue of 1738 brought further improvements in the exactness of entries. In general, progress in cataloguing techniques was restricted almost entirely to Oxford until the nineteenth century was well under way.

The Cambridge University Library has never had a printed catalogue; and, aside from minor compilations of the fifteenth and sixteenth centuries,[79] preparation of its first manuscript catalogue was begun in the eighteenth century. In Scotland and Ireland the first catalogues were printed in the eighteenth century, although the oldest manuscript catalogue had been initiated in 1588 by the Glasgow University Library.[80]

When the older university statutes mentioned library service, it was usually a side line for clergymen. The Oxford statute of 1412[81] speaks of a "chaplain," and this designation was preserved until Bodley's statutes came into force. Thomas James bore the title of protobibliothecarius Bodleianus, and up to the present day his successors have borne the title Bodley's Librarian. Insofar as duties of office were concerned, the learned James, editor of the *Philobiblon*, did not feel himself bound to the schedule fixed by Bodley.[82] Of course, he also had to be satisfied with an annual honorarium of £40, his assistant with £10, and the one servant with £4; and as late as 1789 proposals for far-reaching improvements in salaries failed. Similarly the Cambridge librarians of the sixteenth and seventeenth centuries had to find sources of income other than their miserable salaries. It was little wonder that the library profession could exercise no great attraction and that able men took refuge in professorships or clerical livings, even though there was never a scarcity of applicants for vacant positions. Cambridge[83] was so fortunate as to have Abraham Wheelocke and William Moore as librarians, both of whom were at once scholars of repute and still men who looked upon their office as a most distinguished position. Moore's successor, Thomas Smith, administered the office from 1659 on so well that the university regarded him highly enough to give him the title of Principal Librarian in 1715. In the colleges the master himself was usually able to administer the library in view of the much smaller collections. In the Scottish libraries the professors took over the office of librarian as a side line.

On the other hand, professional librarians administered the private collections of the sixteenth century. Archbishop Parker employed his excellent chaplain, Stephen Batman (died 1584), in this capacity.[84] Cotton was his own librarian, but when the Cotton Library was erected in 1700 Dr. Thomas Smith was employed and after him William Hanbury.[85] In the old Royal Library Patrick Young worked for the three royal bibliophiles, Prince Henry, James I, and Charles I; and under the Commonwealth Bulstrode Whitelocke was installed.[86] John Dury[87] was his deputy from 1649 to 1654.

Dury might be called the first English library theorist, and his ideas were more advanced than those of anyone who had expressed himself on library administration since Richard de Bury, Sir Humphrey Gilbert, or John Dee. Dury, Scottish clergyman and "peacemaker," had set for his goal the reunion of all Protestant sects; and during his wide travels in northern Europe he had come into contact with numerous important and learned men, among others Samuel Hartlib of Elbing, who settled in England in 1628. In two letters to Hartlib dated 1650 Dury developed his occasional thoughts on libraries which Hartlib then published in the tract *The Reformed Librarie-Keeper*.[88] He argued that the librarian must not only care for his books but also show special learning and accomplishments in order to elevate his ill-paid and underrated work. He said that a university library should be the center of scientific and literary interests and that librarians should be guides, advisers, and teachers of the readers. Accordingly, the librarian should maintain correspondence with bookdealers, scholars, and other librarians and a scientific exchange of ideas on an international basis (as one might say today). A group of the most learned doctors should serve him as a library committee and assist him by suggesting acquisitions. He should not decline depository copies but should shelve them in a special place after they are entered in an alphabetical catalogue and the classification noted. Dury recommended printed classified catalogues, showing shelf locations and leaving room for manuscript additions, but omitting less important works. Only responsible work of this sort would justify a proper salary of a hundred pounds, or, even better, two hundred. But these were thoughts which did not reappear until the latter part of the eighteenth century or later.

CHAPTER TWO

FROM THE END OF THE SEVENTEENTH CENTURY TO THE ACCESSION OF VICTORIA

UNIVERSITIES AND INTELLECTUAL LIFE[89]

A new day for English scientific and intellectual life dawned with the restoration of the Stuarts. The universities gradually eliminated the last remnants of Aristotelianism, which had been strengthened by the statutes of Archbishop Laud as late as 1636 and unchallenged by the regulations of 1645 and 1664. Thinkers who had been trained in mathematics and the sciences, like Hobbes, William Dell, John Webster, and even Milton, criticized as sharply as possible the tenacious instructional methods of scholasticism and demanded the introduction of mathematics, science, medicine, and the liberal arts as well as the abolition of the ironclad, pedantic textbook learning. In Oxford, where Sir Henry Savile had occupied the first chair of mathematics as early as 1619, a group of mathematicians and scientists gathered during the Commonwealth. From this group Robert Boyle, John Wallis, John Wilkins, and Christopher Wren, who had joined a society of philosophical inquirers, went to London around 1660 to establish connections with the Royal Society which had just been founded in Gresham College. A final result of the work of this group came in 1677 when Elias Ashmole erected a museum of natural history to which he also presented his valuable library. But Oxford moved gradually into the background, for the methods of instruction deteriorated and petrified more and more until they were reformed at the beginning of the nineteenth century.

It was a different story in Cambridge where a strong tradition of mathematical and scientific learning was established about 1630 and has not been interrupted to the present day. Following the Restoration, the Platonists, enemies of Cartesianism and supporters of

Bacon, were active in Cambridge. The principal adherents were Ralph Cudworth, Henry More, Isaac Barrow, the teacher of Newton, and also the librarian of the University, William Moore. Newton's genius laid the foundations for the development of the exact sciences which unfolded after the beginning of the eighteenth century and were represented by professorships in many universities.

Critical visitors from Germany like the Uffenbach brothers[90] and the Wolffian Professor Christian Gabriel Fischer, of Königsberg who travelled in England in 1710 and 1727-31, have little praise for the status of British scholarship and say nothing good about the use of libraries; but the English universities of that period were by no means inferior to those on the Continent. Indeed English universities were superior to Continental institutions in natural sciences and philological and antiquarian disciplines, the latter being represented by Anthony à Wood, Thomas Hearne, Thomas Tanner, Richard Rawlinson, and William Oldys in Oxford and by Richard Bentley in Cambridge.[91] The long-standing fame of both universities, and not least of all of their libraries, attracted travellers and scholars from all countries throughout the eighteenth century, although native observers, among them none less than Edward Gibbon,[92] criticized academic instruction sharply toward the middle of the century. Indeed, as late as the beginning of the nineteenth century the *Edinburgh Review* announced a book in which an alleged Spaniard expressed himself on the merits of the English universities to the extent of claiming that they were the great schools in which established opinions were inculcated and perpetuated, that Cambridge was of course as much superior to Oxford as Oxford was to Salamanca.[93]

However, it had been a long time since the universities were the only seats of learning and education. After the founding of the Royal Society, more scientific, medical, and philosophical societies were established in the late seventeenth century and throughout the eighteenth.[94] After 1730 industrialism spread over England, and in its wake came the evolution in the national economy from mercantilism to free trade. A profound change in philosophical outlook accompanied this development. What Hobbes and Locke had thought in the seventeenth century was developed with full consistency by

Berkeley and Hume in the eighteenth. Adam Smith and Edmund Burke applied these ideologies to economic, social and political life. The urban middle classes, the merchant, manufacturer, and scholar, assumed their places beside the ruling classes, and the English enlightenment was accepted and broadcast by these groups. Intellectual life of the late seventeenth and eighteenth centuries was reflected in literature, the renascent optimism in the comedies by Dryden, Addison, and Steele, the shady aspects of society in the poetry of Pope and the satire of Swift. The moral and political weeklies like the *Tatler, Spectator, Examiner,* and *Craftsman,* which appeared in the first third of the eighteenth century, and the *Gentlemen's Magazine* (1731) accompanied political, social, and literary events with their frank criticism, which above all held no brief for universities and men of learning.[95] This conjuncture of intellectual and material prosperity also benefited the libraries. The eighteenth century saw the beginnings of the great functional libraries which gradually absorbed the smaller, hitherto independent libraries.

The Libraries of the Universities

In the first decades of the eighteenth century the growth of the Bodleian Library was insignificant. Depository rights brought no great accessions, and only occasionally it received an important gift. But in the second half of the century the rate of growth was doubled, and the value of accessions increased many times. During the librarianship of Humphrey Owen (1747-68) the library was given the collection of Richard Rawlinson (1755) and the Clarendon State Papers (1759),[96] both of which are invaluable source material for modern history. Owen was succeeded in office by John Price and Bulkeley Bandinel, each of whom remained in office for almost a half-century and each distinguished more for antiquarian learning than for administrative ability. Bandinel brought the holdings of the library to 260,000 volumes of printed books and 22,000 manuscripts. In the annals of the Bodleian, 1845 will stand out as a remarkable year, distinguished as the only one in a long history during which the library acquired no manuscript.[97] The first decades of the nineteenth century were particularly favorable for the acquisition of manuscripts and early imprints, for many a private collection had been put on the market stimulated by the great auctions. Towards the middle of the century the Bodleian surpassed more than ever all other libraries of the nation in size and value.[98]

In contrast to the university library, the college libraries had no fixed policy of acquisition. According to Dr. Johnson, who visited Oxford frequently in pursuit of his lexicographical studies, the libraries of All Souls and Christ Church were the most important at the middle of the eighteenth century; and while he had nothing to say about problems of administration and acquisition, neither did he have special interest in them.[99] The university became interested in the college collections for the first time in 1794 when it attempted to make a union catalogue of the collections. However, the project went no further than the preparation of a few lists of holdings.[100]

Still, Oxford had been the chief seat of cataloguing technique throughout the eighteenth century. Hyde's catalogue of 1694 soon showed the need of revision. The revision was based on thorough-going comparisons with the books themselves and corrected numerous errors in the older edition. It appeared in 1738 in two folio volumes and was used until the fifth catalogue of printed books appeared in 1843-51.[101] After 1780 the library published annual lists of accessions which absorbed in 1796 the list of donors begun by Bodley in 1600.

Neither Cambridge nor the Scottish university libraries could show anything comparable to Oxford's accomplishment. In Cambridge there was no organized cataloguing whatsoever in the eighteenth century, and the Scottish libraries were satisfied with manuscript catalogues, although occasional attempts were made to put them in print. Only the Advocates' Library in Edinburgh published a catalogue which appeared in three volumes between 1742 and 1831. After publication it was augmented by manuscript entries.[102] On the whole the eighteenth century was not yet ripe for the science of cataloguing, which had to wait until the next century to be developed by the British Museum.

But if the Cambridge University Library was far behind the sister library in Oxford, it obviously enjoyed the position of favorite with George I, who gave it the famous 30,755 volume collection of Bishop

Moore of Ely in 1715. In view of its riches as well as of its founder it was called the Royal Library.[103] It gave an excuse for expanded quarters which were ready in 1755 and were used for eighty years more.[104] Unlike more conservative Oxford, the members of the university had free access to books and unconditional borrowing privileges, and this practice is still maintained in spite of losses it has caused. The library's income remained as modest as it had been in the seventeenth century, although the library committee took a definite share in the administration and support of the university's library by virtue of a statute of 1748.[105] In some respects the presence of this committee weakened the administration of the library by the principal librarian, but on the whole it strengthened him. Of the five librarians of the eighteenth century Conyers Middleton was the most outstanding. To outsiders he was known for his bitter feud with Bentley which held the entire university breathless. He suffered a well-deserved defeat but earned a moral victory. Within the university his fame rested on his attempt to set up a new classification for the library. To be sure, it was never used, but it did represent one of the first theoretical considerations in this field.[106]

Among the college libraries Trinity, equipped with a magnificent reading room constructed in 1677-92 by Sir Christopher Wren,[107] forged ahead at the beginning of the eighteenth century and has held a leading position ever since. Numerous but relatively insignificant legacies fell to the other college libraries. For example, the library of Corpus Christi received only a portion of Newton's correspondence from his bequest. But rarely has one of the libraries been so fortunate as to receive a well-rounded collection in a gift or a bequest. Magdalene College occupies a peculiar position in this respect with the 3,000 volume collection of Samuel Pepys, less remarkable for its content than for the curious stipulations attending the presentation.[108]

Eighteenth century Scotland was concerned with weightier problems than the cultivation of science and libraries. There were no great collectors and generous philanthropists, and the Stuart bibliophiles tarried beyond the seas. To be sure, Queen Anne had extended depository rights to the university libraries of Edinburgh, Glasgow, and Aberdeen and to the Advocates' Library in 1709;[109] but the delivery must have been a rather haphazard affair, for in 1836 Edinburgh, Glasgow, and Aberdeen frivolously surrendered their rights for annual subsidies of £575, £707, and £320 respectively. Other sources of income consisted partially in graduation and matriculation fees. For example, Edinburgh derived from this source a sum of about £500. The administration of rules for use and lending must have been rather lax up into the nineteenth century; for sharp regulations had to be issued against procrastinating borrowers, among them professors with several hundred volumes. About 1830 the Edinburgh University Library owned 70,000 volumes and was able to occupy a new building with its great reading room, still today one of the most beautiful halls of Scotland. Aberdeen, with 32,000 volumes, remained far behind Edinburgh.[110]

The eighteenth century was a favorable period for the libraries of Ireland. Between 1712 and 1724 Trinity College was able to finish a new building, the noble Long Room, at the cost of £17,000. It was occupied in 1734. But there were no sources of fixed income and consequently no systematic growth, and the library was forced to depend upon gifts.[111] However, gifts were fairly frequent, among them such important collections as those of Sir William Palliser, Archbishop of Cashel (1726), of Dr. Claudius Gilbert (1736), of Dr. John Stearne, Bishop of Clogher (1741), and finally the 20,000 volume collection of Henrick Fagel, secretary of the States General and pensionary of Holland, removed to England during the French Revolution, sold for £9,000, and presented to Trinity College. Here, just as in Oxford and Cambridge, the growing library attracted large and small collections and offered them a place of refuge in uncertain times. In the same year as the legislative union with Great Britain, Trinity College received depository rights for printed works of the United Kingdom.

THE FOUNDING OF THE BRITISH MUSEUM[112]

When Richard Bentley received his patent as keeper of all royal libraries in 1693, he found the old Royal Library[113] in St. James poorly housed and sadly neglected. But his attempts to win royal support for the erection of a new building in St. James' Park and to change the library into a national library failed. Bentley was chosen master of Trinity College in Cambridge and left the business of his office to the deputy keeper, David Casley, while he himself only occasionally exercised superficial administrative duties. Around the turn of the century it was proposed to unite the Royal Library with the Cotton Library,[114] but this proposal was never carried out. George I, according to Dr. Johnson, neither knew anything nor wanted to know anything, and George II showed no initiative whatsoever. However, there was a local union of both libraries when the Cotton Library was moved in 1730 to the Ashburnham House in Westminster, where the Royal Library was also located at the time, but neither was very accessible here and therefore little used. When a fire broke out on October 23, 1731 the Cotton Library was seriously endangered, and it was saved only with loss or damage of 200 manuscripts.[115] Twenty-two years more passed before a decision was reached. In 1752 the curators of the Cotton Library petitioned Parliament for the erection of a suitable building to insure its future availability to the public, arguing that its liberal use had produced the most learned works of its day.

In the following year Parliament approved the purchase of the famous manuscript collection of Robert and Edward Harley, first and second Earls of Oxford. It had been offered by the heiress, the Duchess of Portland, for the relatively small sum of £10,000 on the condition that it be united with the Cotton Library.[116] The decision was hastened by the appearance of a third great collection on the market. The distinguished physician and scientist Sir Hans Sloane had opened in 1741 a museum of art and natural history in his manor house at Chelsea, a suburb of London. It was a point of attraction for the entire world of learning and polite society.[117] In his will (1748) he offered house, museum, and library of 40,000 printed books and 3,500 manuscripts to the public for the sum of £20,000. After Sloane's death the uninterested George II declined the proposition; but through the intervention of the speaker of the House of Commons, Arthur Onslow, an act (26 George II, C. 22) was passed by which the Sloane, Cotton and Harley collections were united to form the British Museum.[118] Since Chelsea lay too far from the center of London, the Montagu House at the outskirts of the city was bought. It was a relatively simple piece of baroque architecture with a central portion and two forward jutting wings whose interior had been reconstructed in 1755-58. On January 15, 1759 the British Museum was opened, and it remained in these quarters until the time of the building program of 1823. The peculiarity of the united collections, the combination of a great library with an art gallery and a curiosity cabinet, seemed at that time natural, even useful. However, it brought from the very beginning a disruption of organization and administration which was revealed in many difficulties involving space as well as proprietary interests. Even the later removal of the natural history collection to South Kensington did not fully eliminate these problems.

In harmony with English regard for legal nicety, the property, administration, and control of the British Museum were handed over to a board of trustees by the Act of Incorporation.[119] The composition of this group corresponded to the private-governmental-public character of the institution. Among those represented were three high public offices, the families of the founders, the crown, scientific corporations, and various men from public life.[120] Of the three principal trustees the Archbishop of Canterbury occupied the first chair and held the leading position. Gradually he acquired control over the formulation of policy and important appointments and decisions. The number of members on the board varied, but in 1835 there were forty-eight. Since this number was too large to permit easy consideration of business in full session,[121] the board established as early as 1755 a standing committee for the disposition of current business and special committees for such questions as books, manuscripts, antiquities, finance, building, and other matters. The number of members of the committees varied, and their qualifications were rather indeterminate. Although the board passed many regulations after 1757 effecting temporary alterations of its structure, the lines of demarcation between the functions of the entire group and the standing committee were so vague that there were constant difficulties and conflicts which were only partially eliminated after 1835 following the reorganization of the administration.

At all events there was no place for a coordinated administrative apparatus in the eighteenth century, and the unstable leadership was also reflected in the library staff. The chief was called the principal librarian, a designation which expressed at the very beginning the superiority of the library over the other divisions. Until 1807 the librarian had to get along with three assistants, a porter, and a messenger; but later more staff members and attendants and after 1827 divisional chiefs were added, until the staff had grown to about eighty members in 1835. After 1805 there was a secretary of the board through whom the disposition of business matters passed. He was given actual though not legally specified authority over the staff members and even the principal librarian. The duties of the librarians were rather indefinite. Originally they consisted of directing visitors, and only when attendants were present were the librarians free to arrange and catalogue books and perform other professional duties. In spite of the rather modest salaries, positions in the British Museum attracted a sufficient number of applicants; and thus it was possible to establish a tradition in acceptance, training, and placement and ultimately to establish a professional caste which has provided scholars and administrative officials for the chief positions up to the present day. Of the four principal librarians of the eighteenth century, Joseph Planta (1799-1827), a native Swiss, was the most important; but the library did not have a professional director until the appointment of his successor, Henry Ellis, who had been trained in the Bodleian.[122]

GROWTH AND USE OF THE BRITISH MUSEUM

The Act of Incorporation had not provided a fixed income for the library of the Museum; and for a half century it depended on occasional gifts and followed an insecure policy of growth. While the functional library at the University of Göttingen was systematically increased by English-Hanoverian appropriations, it was not yet realized in London that a library without a regular, planned program resembles a garden grown wild without the cultivation of a gardener. To be sure, there were generous gifts to the national museum from all corners of the British Empire, but there was always the impression that the library as a whole was not unified. After the first fifty years, careful observers could point to numerous lacunae in the most widely separated fields.[123] It was only in 1784 that the bad habit of shelving gift collections separately was broken. Of the gifts received during the eighteenth century the first, both in time and in content, was the old Royal Library presented lightly and with a royal gesture by George II in 1757 as a birthday gift. A few years later, in 1762, George III added the famous Thomason Collection which he had acquired for the cheap price of £300.[124]

Among the diversified and frequently extremely valuable collections there were numerous documents of the past and treasures thought to have been lost which now came to a final resting place in the national repository. Particularly worthy of note is the Lansdowne Collection which was acquired in 1807 for almost £5,000. It contained invaluable documents and state papers relating to the political and ecclesiastical history of England from Henry VI to George III.[125] This sum was the first appropriation granted by Parliament for acquisition of books, but more came as the occasion arose. In 1812-15 there was even an annual appropriation of £1,000 for strengthening the resources of the library in English history, topography, and antiquities in addition to very considerable grants for purchase of outstanding individual collections.

Together with other English book hunters and book buyers, the British Museum appeared on the Continent during this period, especially among German dealers and collectors, to purchase manuscripts and valuable imprints from the libraries of secularized cloisters. Dibdin reports[126] that the British Museum even negotiated with Baron von Moll for the purchase of a whole castle full of books and manuscripts; and, indeed, a large part of the gigantic collection of von Moll fell into its possession. But the most valuable acquisitions of the nineteenth century were the Banks Library and the King's Library. Joseph Banks, scientist, traveller, and president of the Royal Society, owned a select collection of scientific (especially botanical) literature which was famed as late as Panizzi's day as an unexcelled model of its kind and remarkable for the classified catalogue compiled by Jonas Dryander.[127] In 1820 the library was left to the British Museum, and it was taken over in 1827.

In the next year George IV gave the private library of George III,[128] containing over 60,000 volumes and 19,000 unbound pieces.

His librarian, Frederick Barnard, had collected the books at great cost at English and Continental auctions. George IV would have preferred to sell the entire collection to the Tsar of Russia who was willing to pay £180,000 for it; but interested parties successfully persuaded the king to give the library to the nation, although not before the royal palm was crossed with a *quid pro quo* from an anonymous source. Parliament appropriated the means for the erection of the noble reading room which was named the King's Library and still ranks among the handsomest library halls in the world. After the British Museum made two more significant acquisitions, the Egerton manuscripts in 1829 and the Arundel manuscripts in 1831, it could be ranked in the first line of European libraries with nearly 240,000 volumes.

But to what extent were these large and rich collections available to the public? The British Museum originated as an art gallery and curiosity cabinet, and this characteristic was not immediately altered even by the library, which alone was quite important. At the same time access was made rather difficult by statutes and tradition in contrast with the practice of many Continental libraries.[129] Natives and foreigners alike had to request and call for admission tickets. Frequently they had to wait for weeks for unused tickets, since the tours were limited by fixed personnel and short hours. It was Planta who first abolished this unfortunate custom which had even led to a regular traffic in tickets. He also extended the hours of the library. The reports of visitors were not very complimentary: In 1762 the French traveller P. J. Grosley complained about the uncalled-for haste of the tours, and twenty years later the Berliner Karl Moritz also felt necessitated to scold his German guide (Wendeborn) for the same reason. Even English visitors complained about the unpleasantness of the tours in which they were hurried through rooms where they might have spent a month.[130] After Planta was able to eliminate many sources of irritation, the number of patrons increased greatly, and the reading room, which had been outfitted anew in 1774 with 120 seats, often had to accommodate 200 patrons.[131] Between 1828 and 1838 additions and remodelling were carried out, and by 1852 the old Montagu House was given up and the present building completed.[132] A new spirit also breathed in these new quarters.

CHAPTER THREE

THE FORMATION OF THE FUNCTIONAL RESEARCH LIBRARIES[133]

THE BRITISH MUSEUM AND THE COMMISSIONS OF INVESTIGATION

With the rapid growth of the library and the collections of the museum, imperfections in the organization of the institution as a whole necessarily appeared. The fact that complaints[134] from patrons were publicized and appeared in the press hurt the interests of the library in no way but rather directed the attention of officials to its needs. An aggressive journalist's public criticism of the principal librarian, Henry Ellis, for alleged negligence in the purchase of a French manuscript collection and a basically unimportant incident, the dismissal of an incompetent subordinate,[135] resulted in the formation of a parliamentary commission of investigation in 1835. Composed of members of the House of Commons, trustees, and experts, the commission heard a series of witnesses, officials and patrons of the British Museum. In 1836 it presented to Parliament the result of its investigations.[136]

The sensation of the investigation was the testimony of Antonio Panizzi, a man who had been employed as an assistant since 1831. He expressed himself with such remarkable competence and insight into the real shortcomings of the administration as well as policies to be pursued in the future that the chief interest of the hearings shifted from the museum to the library, and the latter emerged from the contest as the winner and the more important part. The commission could not fail to recognize the fact that most of the faults which had been criticized were traceable to insufficient funds and shortage of personnel and space. However, it also recognized certain deficiencies in the conduct of library business, although no doubt could be cast upon the conscientious work of the librarians and the services of the trustees. Furthermore, it was revealed that the criticism was actually directed at the business affairs and policies of the board more than at the administration of the library. Since most trustees only rarely attended the meetings, decisions on more important matters were gradually shifted to the three principal trustees, in reality to the Archbishop of Canterbury as the *primus inter pares*. Less important matters fell into a sphere of influence governed by the Secretary of the British Museum.

The commission considered it a fundamental disadvantage that the majority of the trustees were high officials, great noblemen, or clergymen, and only in unusual cases scientists or official experts. Indeed, here was a basic problem of English administrative practice, and in this field the Italian Panizzi[137] developed principles which were later splendidly justified. He stated that high functionaries were best fitted to safeguard the Museum's interests on account of their general and specific qualifications as well as their connections. Scholars, he argued, were subjective, intent on gaining authority, dogmatic, and narrow; they would do just the opposite of what the librarians suggested, and even scholars like Faraday or poets like Scott and Southey were not so well qualified as the present trustees; and finally librarians were disqualified because they were unable to attain their ends with hardheaded men of affairs, and it was a perfectly satisfactory solution to give them immediate contact with the trustees.

The commission recommended that the board be expanded by admittance of a few representatives of the arts and sciences, but, in the main, everything remained as it had been. Nevertheless, Panizzi had acquired the permanent confidence of the trustees through his testimony, and from this time on his star was in the ascendant.

The next year Panizzi was named successor to the worthy Henry Baber as director of the most important division of the library, "Keeper of Printed Books." Due to the weak initiative of Henry Ellis it was inevitable that Panizzi should also assume leadership in all affairs of the library. His great purpose was to make the British Museum an archive of national culture, and, even beyond that, of world literature. It was to be neither a show place nor a library of light and ephemeral literature, but a collection of the best and most valuable works of all times and all nations for serious, scholarly research. But this goal was still far distant in 1836.

Solidly founded on Edward Edward's careful compilation of lacunae,[138] Panizzi dismissed absolutely the current notion that the British Museum owned every important book. These lacunae were particularly noticeable in standard German works, and Panizzi had estimated an annual appropriation of £10,000 as the amount necessary to keep step with all desiderata in older and more recent literature. The annual appropriations were increased, but they were still far less than what had been expected.[139] However, from this time on there was scarcely any great auction in England or on the Continent in which the British Museum did not participate directly or indirectly. The American collectors had not yet appeared on the market, and Panizzi employed this period in acquiring for the Museum, with the help of Henry Stevens,[140] the first Americanist, an incomparable collection of Americana and thereby won a start which was never to be overtaken.

The decade of 1837 to 1847 was one of the most fruitful, and even the treasury was less reserved after Panizzi had presented his case on the basis of an extremely careful analysis. He had said that existing lacunae could not be filled by ordinary funds or even gifts but only by extraordinary appropriations of £10,000 annually.[141] Provided with this sum (later reduced to £4,500) at once for the three years, Panizzi went to work and collected systematically in all fields.[142] According to the estimate of the bookdealer Asher, the Museum exceeded all other libraries in the world in respect to its collections of scientific literature and society publications. German literature received especial attention, and the history of European as well as non-European countries was collected only sightly less avidly. British diplomats, agents, and travellers in far lands helped the Museum collect the latter. Among the numerous acquisitions of these years special mention can be made only of the Coptic and Syriac manuscripts of the fifth to thirteenth centuries discovered by Henry Tattam from 1838 to 1842 in the Nitrian monasteries of the Libyan Desert.[143] Further valuable accessions came from the Balkans, Arabia, Persia, and China, although frequently opposition from the trustees and other administrative considerations had to be taken into account. But the handsomest acquisition was the library of the Rt.

Hon. Thomas Grenville, 20,000 volumes valued at £56,000, the finest and rarest works, early imprints and first editions from all fields which this sensitive and generous collector had gathered over a period of thirty years and presented to the British Museum and the nation in 1846 because of his friendship with Panizzi.[144]

The first decade during which Panizzi held office saw a complete reorientation in all branches of library administration. It could not be avoided that the frequently drastic measures aroused misgivings and contradictions. The public, as well, displayed a lively interest in the growth of the Museum, but it was also aware of alleged and actual faults in organization and use. However, behind the criticism was concealed a disinclination toward the Italian, who had now become the soul of the British Museum. Discontent and envy also found expression in the daily press and finally, in March 1847, in a memorandum to the Prime Minister, Lord Russell. Parliament felt compelled to institute a new commission of investigation composed of members of the House of Commons under the chairmanship of the Earl of Ellesmere. It met between June 1847 and May 1849 and subjected the library to a penetrating and extensive examination in many hearings.[145] Again Panizzi was the center of the hearings which often reached dramatic climaxes; but time and again he was able to dispose of the opposition with superior knowledge and irony. The commission was sufficiently open-minded to recognize the justification of Panizzi's measures even when they were contrary to the opinions of experts and the wishes of individual trustees.

The result of the inquiry was a brilliant justification of the policy of the Museum in general and Panizzi in particular, and indeed it was an immediate turning point in the development of library administration. Everyone recognized the competence of the professional librarian. The board of trustees was restricted to a supervisory role, and the actual administration was transferred to the principal librarian and his subordinate professional staff. The majority of the committees, whose composition and function were very indefinite and which were always inclined to interfere with the administration, were reduced to one standing committee and in addition two subcommittees for library and for antiquities respectively. The secretary of the board was once more included in the professional hierarchy

37

and made responsible to the director of the Museum. Appointment of librarians was put back into the hands of the board outside the secretary's sphere of influence.

THE BRITISH MUSEUM CATALOGUE

But the central problem of the commission of investigation was the catalogue of the British Museum, at that time in the process of revision; and the testimony of Panizzi on this point was the beginning of what we call library science.[146] Only the briefest outline of the history of the British Museum catalogue can be given here, but it bears an epochal significance not merely for British librarianship but for the library world in general. The problem of cataloguing had already been discussed in the British Museum soon after the appearance of Harper's two volume folio catalogue in 1771-87, for this work could no longer be considered suitable for the rapidly growing collection in spite of manuscript additions. In 1807-19, Henry Ellis and Henry Baber, both of whom had served their apprenticeship in the Bodleian, published a catalogue in seven octavo volumes. Aside from internal weaknesses and inaccuracies, it was overwhelmed by the holdings twenty years later and had almost no value. After 1836 shelf locations were entered in the reading room copy of this catalogue and patrons had to indicate it on call slips, a move which cut down time required for delivery but not the time consumed in using the catalogue. Errors slipped in because numerous accessions of this period were not entered on the basis of books themselves but rather on the basis of existing catalogues of individual collections. The desire for a revision was also avidly discussed by the public, but opinions on the ideal catalogue varied widely.

It had already been demonstrated with utmost clarity before the commission of 1836 that neither patrons nor experts, neither trustees nor even most of the librarians had a clear conception of the nature of a library catalogue. Among patrons and scholars, obviously influenced by the Dryander catalogue of Banks' collection, a subject catalogue was considered desirable; but opinion within the Museum wavered between a subject catalogue and an alphabetical author catalogue. Panizzi, testifying before the first commission, had clarified conceptions somewhat when he stated from his knowledge of foreign libraries that everywhere cataloguing had begun with inventories, that subject catalogues were good in theory only (with the possible exception of Göttingen), and that even the best subject catalogue could lay no claim to permanence in view of the constant change of scientific systems. On the other hand, he argued, an alphabetical author catalogue would be quite satisfactory if provided with a subject index. In 1833 Baber had presented a new plan for a catalogue which was also attacked and had the basic fault of again making entries according to old catalogues rather than the books. Panizzi had repeatedly pointed out the dangers of this procedure; and as soon as he was made keeper of printed books in 1837, he and his co-workers set up a code for rules of entry. These ninety-one rules, the first in library history, were approved by the trustees in July 1839. With this step the revision of the catalogue was placed on a sound basis for the first time; and it immediately became obvious that previous entries, about 60,000 titles in all, were wrong in many instances and that the earlier method must be discarded at once. While these considerations were still being weighed, the continuation of the work preparatory to printing the new catalogue according to the wishes of the trustees became doubtful.

The differences of opinion on the question of the printed catalogue has contributed a great deal to the clarification of cataloguing theory. Supporters of the printed catalogue, including not only patrons and trustees but also librarians, demanded immediate printing of the first volumes. But Panizzi stubbornly supported his view that it was impossible to begin printing before the entire catalogue was ready from A to Z in manuscript, since otherwise there could be no definitive order and no cross references could be made for anonymous works and works indicating no author. But the trustees firmly demanded immediate initiation of printing and forced Panizzi, in spite of all his representations and against his better judgment, to attempt to begin printing. The A volume (Academies) appeared in 1841 and aroused so much well-merited criticism that the continuation was postponed. Nevertheless, the trustees insisted on seeing the catalogue in print not later than 1844. When Panizzi then set 1854 as the earliest possible date, a decision was avoided, and Panizzi thereupon put an immediate stop to the printing on his own responsibility. The board approved this step in 1846, but Panizzi's enemies tried to force the printing by the subterfuge of the parliamentary committee of investigation. However, even this group supported Panizzi's views in the suit of the Public *vs.* Panizzi, as the *Athenaeum* expressed it. He had maintained that under the existing circumstances the only attainable end was a manuscript catalogue with full titles and extensive cross references. The printing was now postponed for an indefinite period, and the campaign against the Italian ran down with ineffectual protest.

What could not be forced by the opposition of 1850 was finally brought about by the rapid growth of the catalogue itself,[147] for it expanded from 150 volumes in 1850 to 2,250 in 1875 and 3,000 in 1880. The principal librarian at that time, Edward Augustus Bond, and the superintendent of the reading room, Richard Garnett, who was perhaps the most significant figure since Panizzi, calculated for the treasury that the catalogue would soon reach 9,000 volumes and become generally unmanageable. Printing had now become unavoidable and had to be undertaken from A to Z. The treasury was frightened by the necessary expenditure of £100,000 and granted only partial sums, so that Bond felt compelled to print out of alphabetical order and also to close the various letters with different dates, thus publishing with unequal degrees of completeness. Printing began in 1881. Garnett reckoned the period needed for completion as forty years, in approximate agreement with Dziatzko who visited the British Museum at that time, although the latter thought the whole plan was a failure and predicted an impasse in printing after forty years.[148] But Garnett was so successful in stepping up the tempo of printing that the catalogue was completed in 1905 and included all holdings up to 1900.[149] Still, Garnett was thoroughly convinced that only a complete new edition together with supplements would remedy the inequalities in the work as a whole and that a revision should be made every twenty-five years.

RECENT HISTORY OF THE BRITISH MUSEUM

When Panizzi succeeded Sir Henry Ellis in 1856, his principal accomplishments were already history. In 1857 the handsomest external, the new reading room in the courtyard of the Museum building, was opened to the public with 450 seats and a reference collection of 25,000 volumes.[150] The next ten years of his term of office were distinguished less by external success than by the construction of an internal administrative organization. In 1866 Sir Anthony Panizzi retired and lived quietly until April 8, 1879, in the shadow of the British Museum. His successor and trusted co-worker, John Winter Jones, was not so inclined to radical new measures and allowed the fruits to ripen which had been borne in the years of the struggle for administrative reform and the catalogue. During his term of office the reference collection in the reading room was built up, and subject arrangement in 700 groups was introduced in the stacks.[151] There was also an increase in personnel and improvement of salary schedules.

The next administrator, Edward Augustus Bond (1878-88) showed more initiative. He pressed the printing of the catalogue and lists of accessions, the transfer of the natural history section to South Kensington, the building program and other improvements which might have been expected least of all from him, the former chief of the manuscript division. Bond retired in 1888. His successor, Sir Edward Maunde Thompson, who also came up through the manuscript division, completed the building of the newspaper storage building in Colindale (Hendon) to which 48,000 bound volumes were immediately moved and began construction of the north wing of the Museum, which was opened in 1914 as the Edward VII Gallery.[152] Sir Frederick Kenyon followed him in 1910; Sir George Hill was appointed to succeed Kenyon in 1931; and Sir John Forsdyke followed Hill in 1936. Since 1926 the work of the secretary's office has been in the hands of Arundell Esdaile.

The professional staff of the library, now about 250 persons, has been built up since Panizzi's day and consists of an upper group (divisional chiefs, their associates, and assistants) and a lower group (clerks and attendants). It has always been the policy of the British Museum to attract its apprentices from qualified university men and to give them in-service training. A long line of distinguished librarians and scholars, of whom only such names as Richard Garnett,

Coventry Patmore, Edmund Gosse, and Robert Proctor may be mentioned, confirm the value of this method. The government of the British Museum has remained fundamentally as it was in Panizzi's day.[153] However, the right of appointment vested in the principal trustees has become merely advisory, and the decision lies with the Civil Service Commission and the Director of the Museum (principal librarian), himself appointed by the crown.

The board of trustees no longer controls any funds except endowments, which now pale into relative insignificance beside the annual appropriation granted by the treasury on the recommendation of the board of trustees. Since the last great donation, the Grenville collection, regular appropriations have permitted systematic though not overabundant increase of holdings, which now include over 4,500,000 printed books, 55,000 manuscripts, about 2,400 papyri, and 84,000 pieces of records. Garnett has said that the growth represents a much more diversified collection than was revealed by the holdings of 1857, for it reflects at once the events of the time and the wealth of England.[154] The British Museum has developed into a national library, which lends no books for outside use according to its act of incorporation, but which occupies the most distinguished position in the British system of national libraries by virtue of the value of its holdings, its accessibility through the catalogues, and its directors.

The Libraries of the Universities: Oxford and Cambridge

About the middle of the nineteenth century the reformation of the universities began, heretofore exclusive preserves of the High Church and the moneyed classes.[155] A beginning had already been made with the founding of University College in London in 1826, independent of clerical associations, although the Anglican King's College was established in 1831 as a counterinfluence. The industrial and commercial development of the nation furthered this tendency, for it resulted in improved technical education and increased attendance at the universities. In Oxford and Cambridge there were movements to do away with the religious monopoly, to modernize the administration as well as methods of instruction and research, and to strengthen the position of the university against the colleges with respect to finances. These purposes were attained in part by the Oxford and Cambridge Act of 1877.

More successful were the movements in northern England where new universities, predominantly dependent on state appropriations and emphasizing applied rather than exclusively humanistic curricula, were founded in the eighties on the basis of the technical colleges which already existed. For Scotland as well, new, modern constitutions strongly reminiscent of the American universities were introduced by royal acts of 1858 and 1889. In Ireland the law of 1873 purported to make Trinity College into a national university for the whole land; but it remained the representative of the Episcopal Church, and therefore Queen's College was established by its side in 1879 as the Catholic university of Ireland together with a Presbyterian university in Belfast. The university reforms influenced the development of the libraries to such an extent that they were made agencies of the university as a whole and were financed by state appropriations.[156] The royal commissions and the reform committees of Oxford and Cambridge also took up the question of relations of the college libraries with one another and with the university library. In view of the extensive but unregulated nature of book collections in all universities, this question has been solved no better in Great Britain than in Germany and the United States.

In Oxford the royal commission of 1850[157] made two proposals for the Bodleian Library, relaxation of the prohibition against outside lending and closer cooperation with the college libraries. Opinion within the university concerning the propriety of outside loans was divided, for the advantages of the system in such institutions as Cambridge, Edinburgh, and Göttingen could be answered with an equal number of disadvantages. Accordingly the commission proposed a compromise: restriction of outside borrowing to certain professors, unrestricted lending of duplicates, lengthening of hours, and establishment of a new reading room and reference collection for undergraduates. Consideration was given to further proposals such as removing from college libraries to the Bodleian those books which were not in the latter and could be spared by the former, a union catalogue, and reciprocal privileges. The only practical result of these proposals was the establishment of a reading room with a reference collection for undergraduates in the Radcliffe Camera in 1862.[158] Violent opposition was aroused against outside lending. Even though the Bodleian statutes were changed in 1873[159] to permit outside lending to all members of the university, this provision was allowed to stand only until 1887 and in 1888 was even abrogated for corporate bodies within the university.

In 1871 an attempt was made to limit fields in which books were to be collected. Various college libraries were to emphasize only special fields, while the Camera was to secure much-used texts and reference works and the Bodleian expensive and rare books. Even this plan was not realized until much later, in 1927-29, when a few libraries were made subordinate to the curator of the Bodleian and thereby subjected to the narrower cooperative relationship proposed earlier.[160] Among other plans worthy of mention was the proposal put forward at the London International Library Congress of 1877 relative to the consolidation of the important libraries of All Souls and Queen's with the Bodleian. The large income of Queen's was to be given to the Bodleian.[161] This plan, which was also supported by the press, was killed by the opposition of the House of Commons during the discussion of the University Bill; and the only result of it was that All Souls legal library was made accessible to the whole university, even for outside loans. The other colleges have done no more than to permit general use and outside loans only to their own members, including undergraduates, and to introduce a limited system of reciprocity. Ever since the beginning of the twentieth century, Oxford University has faced the difficult problem of making effective use of a constantly growing mass of books in the Bodleian as well as in many college libraries for members of the university and research workers in general. It was only on the basis of the 1931 university commission's work that a solution was found, and a large scale plan was set up which was to be completed by the Bodleian expansion.[162]

Outside loans and cooperation had been apparently insoluble problems in Oxford, but not so in Cambridge. The university commission of 1852 found the libraries sufficiently accessible, and accordingly it considered only the memorandum of the librarian, John Power, for a more effective administration and better organization

of the university library.[163] The commission showed enough insight to recommend a stronger position for the director in relation
not only to the excessively large and unworkable library committee
but also to his staff. One unsatisfactory condition was the absence
of a reading room due to the policy of open access. Power's predeces-
sor, John Lodge, had begun with a classified arrangement of the
books but had only created considerable disorder. Power wisely
heeded advice from his colleagues in Oxford and the British Museum and decided that a large, rapidly growing library could not be
satisfactorily classified and accordingly stopped Lodge's project. Testifying before the commission he supported the modern idea that
the serious patron will not be guided by the shelving of books but
rather by bibliographies and references and that therefore a well-
made catalogue with precise locations was necessary. Accordingly,
Cambridge has never gone back to a classified arrangement but
rather has used a chronological-alphabetical method of shelving.[164]
Consistent with his evaluation of the catalogue as a library tool,
Power wanted to concentrate use in a reading room with a large reference collection and avoid work in the stack and outside loans. In
1854 Power also began the main alphabetical catalogue, provided
with printed entries after the model of the British Museum catalogue, and he completed the printing of the catalogue of manuscripts.

Power's measures had their full effect under his successor, Henry
Bradshaw, a man whose personality and accomplishments shaped
the destiny of the university library for the twenty years between
1867 and 1886.[165] His term of office was distinguished less by administrative accomplishments than by the scholarly spirit which
permeated the library and made it the center of instruction and research in Cambridge. Thanks to Bradshaw's extraordinary competence in the field of manuscripts and incunabula as well as in the
Oriental and Celtic languages, Anglo-Saxon, and early English dia-
lects, the library had thoroughly reorganized and catalogued manuscripts and incunabula as early as 1867. His academic reputation,
trips to the Continent, and to the libraries of the most important
European countries brought him into close contact with other librarians and scholars. The great personal esteem which he enjoyed
within the university contributed not merely to the library's growth

but, above all, to its use. Even Mommsen, who visited Cambridge in 1885 to clarify doubts about a work ascribed to Gildas, felt that he was richly rewarded by Bradshaw's assistance and personality.[166]

Bradshaw did not have Panizzi's talents for organization. Only a few of his measures, for example, the method of accession and the arrangement of the shelving in the stacks, were of permanent value, whereas his inclination to bother about all details prevented him from exercising broad supervision and summoned forth much disorder.[167] Of course, healthy development of the library was prevented by chronically crowded quarters, a condition not perceptibly improved by the building program begun in 1837 and completed by Bradshaw. The collection grew rapidly in the last quarter of the nineteenth century and first quarter of the twentieth. What with heavy endowments and large gifts, for example, the 20,000 volume collection of Lord Acton, the library constantly threatened to burst not merely through its walls but also through the frame of the staff organization. This problem was not solved until the magnificent new library building was constructed in the years 1930-34.

THE LIBRARIES OF THE UNIVERSITIES: LONDON AND THE NORTH[168]

London University was formed in the course of the nineteenth century by a rather loose consolidation of a large number of originally independent colleges and other institutions. In this broad frame there were, besides the three large libraries (King's College, University College, and the University), numerous smaller libraries for both general and special purposes, among them the medical collections of the hospitals, historical, linguistic, and philological collections, and in addition to all these the important and diversified library of the London School of Economics. All these libraries spread out over the city considered themselves independent units and even failed to realize closer relations when the University of London was reorganized in 1900 by uniting the two old colleges and not less than twenty-nine other institutions into a complicated university. It can hardly be said that all these libraries belonging to the university were able to agree on a common policy. However, the larger libraries, namely, those of the University, University College, and King's College, became central depots for branch and departmental libraries; and among these three some cooperation in regard to reciprocal accessibility and lending was attained with government assistance.

Of the three groups, the University Library[169] is probably the best unified. It arose from various larger and smaller foundations that were gradually amalgamated and received in 1903 the most significant part of its holdings in the 60,000 volume economics collection of Professor H. S. Foxwell which was purchased by the Goldsmiths' Company and presented to the university. The group belonging to the University College[170] offered greater problems. In addition to a number of individual collections, for example the libraries of Bentham and Ricardo, which were housed in a special building since 1848, there have been up to the present time gifts and endowments from the many different sources, all of which were put together to form the General Library. Side by side with this library more or less independent seminar collections arose in a similar fashion, among them, for example, that of the School of Librarianship, all in their own quarters, freely accessible, and with provisions for study desks and outside lending. They served the students of the Liberal Arts College and were grouped together under the designation of Arts Libraries. Another group was formed by collections in technology and science which were united with the Science Library, the individual medical collections, and the deposit copies of various society libraries, which in 1914 had grown to more than 250,000 volumes. A final group of some 70,000 volumes (1910) in various fields had been formed in and around King's College Library.[171]

If it was difficult to attain a common policy of administration, finance, and acquisition within each of these groups, it was so much more so within the university as a whole. At all events in London, for the first time in England, a successful attempt (not without American influence) was made to regulate the relations between university, college, and seminar libraries. Each of the groups of libraries connected with the two colleges was placed under the central authority of the librarian and the library committee, and they were to serve primarily as reference, research, and seminar libraries. The group of libraries belonging to the University supplements the other two in acquisition and lending. The patrons of one group are also granted lending privileges in the others according to the special regulations of the library concerned. By these amalgamations London was able to avoid the error committed in Germany of permitting the university and seminar libraries to exist side by side with no provision for reciprocity and without sufficient funds. The London School of Economics,[172] founded in 1896, was also drawn into London University's sphere of influence. Its splendid collection, the British Library of Political and Economic Science, likewise consists of a group of individual collections and valuable gifts of private collectors.

The new universities of the North[173] were organized after the fashion of London. As young institutions they needed state appropriations and were therefore subjected to more state control than the older universities. They have the difficult task of forming a link between science, capitalism, and middle classes. Like the universities themselves, the libraries are of recent origin, and they represent the modern fields of research, among which natural and social sciences and technology are strong but not the only fields. Just as in London, individual collections are more or less closely linked with the university library.

CHAPTER FOUR

THE FORMATION OF THE
FUNCTIONAL PUBLIC
LIBRARIES

STATE, ENDOWED, AND CORPORATION LIBRARIES

In the eighteenth century learning and scientific research were not restricted to the universities. Indeed, as early as the second half of the eighteenth century the sciences had found a refuge in Gresham College, the seat of the Royal Society.[174] The corporations of physicians and lawyers go back to an even older period. In the eighteenth century societies and academies began to blossom forth,[175] and during the nineteenth century, especially in London, they developed with almost inconceivable prolificacy in the sciences, technology, and numerous other fields. From the middle of the eighteenth century on there arose literary and philosophical societies and the royal societies, academies, institutes, or whatever they pleased to call themselves, cultivating literary, historical, or artistic interests. All these scientific and professional corporations established libraries supported by membership fees and endowments. Originally their use was limited to members, but latterly they have been made increasingly accessible to research workers, students, and a restricted public. Their holdings were reckoned in tens-of-thousands, and individual libraries passed the hundred-thousand mark. The more valuable portions of the holdings consisted largely of the corporations' own publications and exchanges from foreign societies, but nearly all owned rare or unique collections in one or another special field. The National Library of Ireland grew out of the library of the Royal Dublin Society,[176] which was taken over by the government of southern Ireland in 1877.

The most important legal library in the nation grew out of the corporation library of the Scottish Faculty of Advocates in Edinburgh, and it became the National Library of Scotland after it was granted depository rights in 1709.[177] It had been founded in 1682 and richly furnished by the Lord Advocate, Sir George Mackenzie of Rosehaugh. At an early period it began to specialize in Scottish literature and history. Towards the middle of the eighteenth century, when none less than David Hume was librarian,[178] the holdings numbered 30,000 volumes. A century later the numerical statistics but not the administration of the library showed improvement, for the funds of the corporation were insufficient to insure satisfactory administration and housing. Early attempts to place the library in the hands of the state failed, although even Thomas Carlyle advocated the step vigorously. It was only when Sir Alexander Hamilton gave his generous endowment of £100,000 after World War I that the long-sought goal was attained. By a law of August 1925 the collection of 750,000 volumes was made the National Library of Scotland. But the building problem was still unsolved, for two other libraries, the Library of the Writers to the Signet (1755) and a smaller library of the solicitors in the highest courts had been housed together with the Advocates' Library in a building complex belonging to the Scottish Parliament. Thanks to another gift of Sir Alexander and to state funds, the National Library is now looking forward to the construction of its new home.[179]

The third national library on British soil is the National Library of Wales in Aberystwyth[180] which was founded in 1873 and became a national library in 1909. However, the component elements descend in part from an earlier period and represent a very complete collection of Welsh literature. The library in Aberystwyth was more fortunate than her sister in Edinburgh. In 1937 it moved into a new building, whose cornerstone had been laid in 1911, with more than 750,000 volumes, 18,000 manuscripts, and 180,000 pieces of records and other documents.

The great national libraries represent at once a beginning and an end: a beginning insofar as each of them came into existence as a public, functional research library, and an end insofar as all were the last means of preserving the great private libraries of an earlier period. As early as the eighteenth century and first quarter of the nineteenth many famous collections had either gone this way or been scattered to the four winds at the great London auctions. Typical examples were the sales of the collections of the Duke of Roxburghe in 1812, of William Beckford in Fonthill in 1823, and of Richard Heber in 1834-37.[181] Only a few private collections and family libraries survived the nineteenth century. Towards the end of the century the most important trade in valuable books had shifted from England to America. The American, Charles A. Cutter, found about 1890 that English private libraries had stopped adding to their collections almost completely.[182] Even the famous Althorp Library had not purchased a book for fifty years. An exception was the library of the Earls of Crawford and Balcarres in Haigh Hall. Founded by their ancestors, the Lords Lindsay, in the sixteenth century, it comprised 100,000 printed books and 6,000 manuscripts by the end of the nineteenth century, and its content was said to represent the best that had ever been thought and known.[183] The manuscripts of the Bibliotheca Lindesiana were given to the John Rylands Library in Manchester in 1901 as the Crawford manuscripts; and none other than its owner, the Earl of Crawford, had stated in a speech before the Library Association three years earlier that the inevitable fate of the great family libraries was absorption by public libraries.

About the same time the Althorp Library of Lord Spencer, justly called the richest private collection in Europe, met this fate.[184] Founded in 1788 and augmented by purchases at all the important auctions and by acquisition of whole collections, the Bibliotheca Spenceriana was expanded after 1812 by the bibliographer Thomas Frognall Dibdin to a library of about 40,000 volumes. It was second to none in the completeness and rarity of its early imprints and the splendor of its manuscripts, and it possessed the finest and rarest editions in all fields. After it was placed on sale in 1892 and was already in danger of being sent across the Atlantic, it was bought by Mrs. Rylands in 1899 and presented to the city of Manchester together with the building and other generous donations in honor of her husband. That the John Rylands Library[185] is wont to be called the British Museum of the North indicates the extent to which this library has developed as a center of scholarly research.

Finally, the London Library[186] should be mentioned at this point.

Founded in 1841 principally upon the insistence of Carlyle as an obvious counterpart in Panizzi's British Museum, it has been more successful than most subscription and club libraries and has developed into one of the most important functional libraries of the capitol.

THE FORERUNNERS OF THE PUBLIC LIBRARIES

Before the middle of the nineteenth century England had no libraries open to the general public such as the German cities had founded after the Reformation. Likewise the English grammar schools of the sixteenth century and the public schools which sprang from them in the seventeenth and eighteenth centuries, founded with quite considerable libraries, were separated from the people by a much broader gap than has ever been the case with the German *Ratschulen* and classical *Gymnasia*.[187] Public instruction was abandoned to the miserable parochial schools, and reading material was limited to didactic tracts and the most elementary handbooks. On the other hand, many church and parsonage libraries which were intended for the lower clergy revealed as early as the seventeenth and eighteenth centuries a notable trend toward providing ministers' families with better reading matter and thereby instruction which the common schools could not give.[188] In 1699 the Scottish minister James Kirkwood wrote a remarkable tract in which he proposed the idea of founding public libraries in all parsonages of the realm, thus anticipating the later conception of the free public library.[189] He even succeeded in establishing seventy-seven libraries with a fund of 12,000 Scottish marks which he had collected in London, persuading the Church of Scotland to provide for their administration, growth, cataloguing, and use, and inspiring a law of 1709 for the establishment of libraries in parsonages.[190] But the Scottish rebellion and the defeat of the Young Pretender in 1749 with the resultant political and social confusion put a stop to this promising development. A statistical investigation of 1828 revealed only a few pitiful remnants.[191]

Almost contemporaneously with Kirkwood the English minister Dr. Thomas Bray had started the parochial library movement with the help of influential friends. Originally founded for the clergy and for spreading religion in the colonies, they soon became generally accessible, and in 1708 a law was passed with provisions for their supervision, cataloguing, and use.[192] In spite of the promotion of Bray's idea by his associates, these libraries enjoyed no better fate than Kirkwood's, for statistical investigations of 1850 and 1877 showed only a few remnants in public libraries, private ownership, or in secondhand bookstores. In Ireland the Archbishop of Armagh, Narcissus Marsh, had founded a "library for the public use" in 1713 and furnished it with a regular income and the valuable collection of Bishop Stillingfleet of Worcester (1699).[193] This public (but in no sense popular) library numbered 15,000 volumes by the end of the eighteenth century. It was reckoned among the best and most accessible in the country and counted Swift and Burke among its patrons. In the nineteenth century it was amalgamated with other collections to form the Dublin Public Library.

Towards the end of the eighteenth century and in the first decades of the nineteenth the need for books and general education made itself felt among social classes created by the nascent industrial revolution. In addition these classes were those to whom the rising prosperity of the country afforded the time and means to satisfy cultural needs. However, the existing arrangements for general and formal education were by no means satisfactory, for municipal and other local government agencies showed a traditional conservatism in such matters. Accordingly, schools and libraries in particular were forced to two characteristic Anglo-Saxon solutions, philanthropy and self-help, both of which attempted to take the place of organized public support. In passing we should note significant attempts in these decades to create opportunities for free schools and free libraries. Leading proponents were Joseph Lancaster and Andrew Bell,[194] the Scottish Provost Samuel Brown of Haddington[195] with his "itinerating libraries," and two London clergymen who founded small reading rooms and lending libraries in thickly populated slums.[196]

Somewhat more backward, however, and of immediately practical import were the institutions created at that time for the instruction and continued education of craftsmen and mechanics. The first mechanics' institute, which later became the important Technical

College of Glasgow (1886), was created in 1823.[197] It grew out of lectures given by Professor George Birkbeck after 1800 at the Andersonian Institute of Glasgow, and it was supplemented by a small library. Glasgow's example was imitated in Edinburgh and in the industrial northern part of England, but above all in London, where Birkbeck himself founded six of these institutes in 1834. The courses as well as the libraries were supported by voluntary contributions, and the latter were administered by the members themselves. Both found such approval among craftsmen and skilled laborers that by 1850 there were 400 of them and 300 more by 1863. Many of their libraries contained several thousand volumes. However, they were not permanent institutions, since they were later taken over by the technical colleges which blossomed forth in the latter part of the century, by the larger municipal trade schools, or by public libraries.

The Founding of the Public Libraries[198]

Toward the middle of the nineteenth century the time was ripe for a system of public libraries. In sharp contrast with the history of popular libraries on the Continent, their development did not follow the lines of popular education or even philanthropy. Instead, they aimed at the purpose of providing serious books for the educated reading public of the cities. The pioneer in this new field was Edward Edwards. As early as 1836 he had proposed to the British Museum commission that the duplicates of that institution be used for founding a public lending library in London, which was in no way conceived as a *popular* library. In 1847, armed with extensive statistical material, he had pointed out to the second commission that London occupied a position inferior to any large European city in this respect. Shortly thereafter he developed his ideas and demands in a widely discussed lecture before the London Statistical Society,[199] and by his enthusiasm he won the attention and approval of the social reformer and politician William Ewart. Together with Joseph Brotherton, Ewart had pushed the Museum Act of 1835 through the House of Commons. Quite similar to Edwards' later proposal, this law regulated municipal art collections and libraries and resulted in the opening of the first institution of this kind in Salford near Manchester.[200]

Ewart now took up Edwards' proposal and succeeded, in August 1848, in getting a parliamentary commission to investigate the question of free public libraries. The whole situation of libraries in Great Britain and Europe at the time was extensively discussed before this commission, which depended chiefly on the material gathered by Edwards, although it also invited recognized experts from other countries to testify. The final report,[201] the magna charta of public libraries, was submitted on July 23, 1849, and accepted Edwards' demands. It recommended the founding of public libraries with unrestricted access, supported by fixed taxes and appropriations and supervised by local committees, in cities as well as rural and industrial districts. Above all, they were to be open in the evening, and they should be reference as well as lending libraries. Their contents were to be made accessible by printed catalogues. The law introduced by Ewart on the basis of this report provided for allowing communities to apply a halfpenny of the pound of basic tax returns for the erection and maintenance of library buildings (but not for acquisition of books!). Not without difficulties and procrastinations by opponents of the reform-minded Ewart, the bill was passed on July 30, 1850, as the Public Libraries Act,[202] with a restriction making it applicable only to cities of 10,000 or more.

The passage of the Public Libraries Act came in a time of strong tensions. Middle-class and parliamentary liberalism inspired by the teachings of Adam Smith, Bentham, Cobden, Malthus, and Ricardo, the industrial and commercial spirit of Manchester, the notions on free trade, and the rising prosperity of the country all resulted in important changes in social structure. Schools and libraries were symptoms of progress as well as of the democratization of education. In 1854 library laws were adopted for Scotland and Ireland.[203] In the same year Scotland dropped the minimum population restriction, and England followed suit in 1867. Other effective aids to the library movement were the Gladstone-Forster school law of 1870, which made communities responsible for the establishment of schools, and the law of 1876, which introduced compulsory attendance and thereby prepared an increasing reading public from year to year.[204] The public library movement made headway in the industrial cities of the North and enjoyed its initial as well as its greatest successes in this region. By 1877 seventy-seven cities had founded public libraries. The Victorian Jubilee was the inspiration for establishing many more, and by the end of the century 360 municipalities had libraries. By the outbreak of World War I there were 600 libraries founded under the library laws.[205]

The Public Libraries Act had an adoptive character,[206] that is, it was binding on the municipalities only when they adopted taxes in the amount prescribed by law. The community was the proprietor and the administrative authority. It set up rules and regulations for the library and could delegate its authority to a duly appointed library committee. Originally the central government maintained a supervisory authority over the public libraries, but later it was surrendered according to the law of 1887 to the Local Government Board, the organ of municipal home rule. By a new library law of 1892, which consolidated or rather repealed the gradually increasing confusion of the laws and regulations, the smaller cities and parishes were also defined as library districts, and smaller districts were permitted to combine to form larger ones. This law became the principal one for England and Wales,[207] and laws of similar content were passed for Scotland in 1894 and 1899 and for Ireland in 1901. Up to the present time sixty-six major and minor library laws have been passed in the United Kingdom.

It soon became evident that the restriction of income to a small fraction of tax receipts was the greatest hindrance to a healthy development. In many communities library income amounted to less than £50 annually, and others had to be satisfied with £20 or even £10.[208] Even the basic law of 1892 had still permitted the "penny-rate" to stand. Only the great industrial cities had freed themselves from this restriction,[209] and in the seventies their libraries had incomes of several thousand pounds. As late as 1900 tax rates rarely amounted to more than a halfpenny, perhaps because public libraries were still valued far less by the people in general than were public schools and other municipal institutions. It was only after World War I that the combined efforts of the Library Association, the Carnegie Trust, and the Adult Education Committee succeeded in pushing through the law of December 20, 1919, which abolished the penny limit generally.[210] However, the results still fell short of what was necessary, for, in general, the finances of the muncipalities still do not apportion to libraries more than 1 per cent of total expenditures.[211]

Nature and Function of the Municipal Library[212]

The English public library not only arose a half century earlier than the German popular library, but also it was developed under basically different conditions and forms. From the very beginning both cultivated the purpose of spreading popular literature and thereby education to all classes of the people who previously had had no access to the nation's cultural institutions. But this inherent didactic tendency of the movement has also given a peculiar Anglo-Saxon character to the organization and policy of the public library and has caused it to assume functions which in other European countries have always belonged to the realm of education and popular cultural institutions but not to libraries. It lay in the very nature of the public library soon to spread its field of activity over the whole area of the city in order to meet the requirements of a rapidly growing public. Manchester (founded 1852) was the first municipal library to open its doors under the Public Libraries Act,[213] and as early as 1857 it had established branches.[214] Other large cities such as Liverpool and Birmingham[215] followed suit and surrounded their central libraries with a ring of branches and deposit collections. These branches were suited to the social groups and social classes within the population. Ultimately they also extended their lending service beyond the city limits to smaller neighboring communities and the countryside beyond. These extensions were accompanied by a progressive departmentalization of activities. There arose special collections and special departments for local history, art, commerce and technology, some in the main building, some in branches. In addition there were departments for newspaper readers, young people, and even children, all of which belong today among the most obvious accoutrements of the public library in the large and medium cities.[216]

The didactic mission of the libraries was expressed in ever more refined reference and advisory services, in cooperation with both lower and higher schools, and above all in participation in the adult education movement.[217] Efforts in the direction of adult education, characteristic for a nation with a relatively weak public school system, were actually much older and had already been expressed and propagated in the mechanics' institutes, in the "working men's colleges" (toward the middle of the century), and in numerous other philanthropic institutions. The movement spread over the whole country with the "labour colleges" and the "polytechnics" of the eighties and nineties, the London Toynbee Hall movement (1884), the Young Men's Christian Associations, and finally the Workers' Education Association founded by Albert Mansbridge in 1903. Toward the end of the century adult education found an associate in university extension, a movement coming out of the old universities which tried to bridge the gap to the nonacademic classes of the population with evening courses, lectures, discussion hours, and propagation of technical literature. The movement was well supported by a similar action program, "library extension," which was supported by popular as well as research libraries.[218] In this instance it was the large municipal libraries in particular which took an active part in adult education with exhibitions and tours, establishment of special reading rooms as well as special collections and travelling libraries, publication of catalogues and reading lists, and their own lectures and courses. After World War I this movement, with its strong sociological and pedagogical bent, found new fields of activity and extended its work to factories, docks, ships, barracks, hospitals, etc.

Stanley Jast has rightly characterized this aspect of the public library's work, which is paralleled only in America, as a purely Anglo-American contribution to civilization.[219] The fact that even the old research libraries have played their role in library extension shows that the nature of the public library is inadequately characterized by the adjective "popular." It would be possible to speak of a "uniform library" if a rather sharp differentiation in holdings as well as clientele had not been formed over a period of years. The public library, at least the larger variety, has two basic aspects, a popular side and a general research side. The Manchester Public Library, whose first librarian was none less than Edwards, had from the very beginning, side by side with the circulation division, a so-called "consulting library," the prototype of the later reference collection. It was a selected collection of handbooks and reference works which were not subject to loan.[220] This type of reference collection was established in all the larger public libraries and equipped with reference books, bibliographical works, and research tools selected according to special and local conditions. Special collections were also frequently delegated to this research department of the library, and accordingly most of the more serious use of the library was concentrated here. When, after 1917, the great municipal libraries created "technical and commercial libraries," these collections soon became a gathering place for patrons interested in business and the applied sciences.

This duality naturally presented many difficulties for the public library. The circulation departments and, as a rule, the branches gradually fell more and more under the influence of the demand for popular material after the introduction of the system of free access by J. D. Brown in 1894.[221] There were times and places where fiction represented 80 per cent of the total circulation. For example, the London public libraries reported this figure in 1894;[222] and even in 1927 official statistics established the fact that 66 per cent of the holdings of circulation departments was fiction and literature and that this class accounted for 78 per cent of the circulation.[223] But the reference collection was endangered by rapid superannuation of the holdings whose acquisition was, in addition, expensive and not so easy to justify as popular literature in the eyes of taxpayers and library committees. Nevertheless, the large municipal libraries consistently maintained the policy of struggling against an overabundance of fiction and of building up the reference and special collections. The validity of this policy, necessitated by the absence of local and national interlibrary loan if by nothing else, is now no longer questioned; and neither can it be doubted that the reference libraries of the great cities with their general and special research collections are often centers of bona fide research. No university can boast of a Shakespeare collection comparable to that of the Birmingham Public Library with its 20,000 volumes in this field.[224] It was natural that the municipal library should have become the leader of the public library movement with its multifarious outgrowths. It must be granted that it has performed a service for administrative techniques, promoted development of professional education and architectural design, and prepared for the formation of a national library system by the new methods of cooperation.

SPECIAL LIBRARIES

Special collections are as old as libraries themselves. In English libraries of the older period they were basic elements of the general collection and in many instances have retained to the present day their special nature in respect to administration. We shall not discuss these collections here, but rather those libraries which have arisen with specialized institutions for scientific, cultural, industrial, and political purposes. The historic libraries of the professional corporations of lawyers, physicians, and clergymen have already been discussed. But aside from these and other forerunners, the special library was a child of the late nineteenth century, and its birthplace was London. Unrivalled by any other city in the nation, the English metropolis was the central point of intellectual, aesthetic, and industrial interests. Its activities, which reached out into all aspects of life, summoned forth a countless number of private, communal, and state institutions, quite as variegated and incalculable as the life and administrative mechanism of the great city itself. London became the greatest library center in the world;[225] and when the guide to London libraries describes some 660 libraries of importance, well over half fall into the category of special libraries.

No attempt can be made here to describe this development, and one must be satisfied with the general observation that in nearly all fields valuable, often unique collections have been put together which are not duplicated in the great libraries either in extent or in individuality. Thus, as a whole, they form a valuable supplement to the great libraries, and all the more so in that they are readily available for serious research insofar as they were not primarily created for popular use. For example, this is the case with the extremely rich library of the Victoria and Albert Museum[226] which was opened in

1887, and with its scientific counterpart, the natural history section of the British Museum, which was moved to South Kensington in 1880.[227] Even the official libraries of municipal and state bureaus are accessible under special conditions; and it is scarcely necessary to point out that in the uncommonly rich collections of the Public Records Office (1838), the India Office (1801), the Foreign Office (1782), or the Colonial Institute (1868) entire epochs of British and world history have found depositories. Even the libraries of political and social clubs, to mention the polar opposite of public libraries, often possess collections which have had their part in the intellectual life of London. Such, for example, are the Athenaeum Club and the Reform Club of the Victorian Era.[228]

The youngest special libraries are those for technology and industry, which, to be sure, were foreshadowed by the libraries of the mechanics' institutes. The oldest technological library which was public in the true sense of the word was founded in 1855 for the Patent Office.[229] It was soon distinguished by its wealth of technological periodicals and its almost unlimited generosity in admitting patrons. Two years later the Science Museum was founded in South Kensington and with it a library for technology and related sciences, the Science Library.[230] After it took over the library of the Geological Museum in 1882, it developed into a national library for study and research and became the most important collection of technological literature in Great Britain with more than 200,000 volumes and over 9,000 periodicals currently received. Efforts directed towards the founding of technological libraries were given a new impetus when, as a result of the Technical Education Act of 1889, the system of technological instruction fell to state regulation and the polytechnics and technical colleges were opened. The newer universities of northern England, in particular, set themselves to the task of encouraging technology with special collections and seminar libraries. Even in the older universities collections arose for the engineering sciences. The Scottish university libraries own considerable collections, and even in Oxford and Cambridge the applied sciences and technology have also been cultivated in recent years. The technical colleges with academic standing have given their libraries necessary attention only at a relatively late date. The sole exception is Glasgow, whose library is not only the oldest (1796), but also the most important technological library of Scotland.[231] One of the best and at the same time one of the youngest technological libraries of England is that of Armstrong College in Newcastle-upon-Tyne (1893), which also deserves attention for its modern innovations.[232]

But the college libraries did not bring decisive progress in the formation of the special technological libraries. When World War I revealed the supreme importance of technology and technological literature, the public libraries were the first to understand the exigencies of the times. In the great industrial cities of northern England and Scotland as well as in Bristol and Cardiff special libraries for technology, industry, and finance were created. Housed either in the building of the main library or in buildings of their own, they soon attained great importance.[233] Local industries used their books and services and made agreements with them establishing a mutual relationship in respect to information service, lending, and exchange. Sheffield was a model example. In Manchester, where the technological division (founded in 1922) rose to almost 70,000 volumes in the first decade of its existence, Stanley Jast developed a wholly new technique adapted to the needs of a special library and helped to create a new type of librarian trained in the peculiar problems of special literature, the "special librarian."

Under the pressure of war, British industries had also progressed to the establishment of their own research institutes and libraries with governmental aid. After 1916 the most important national industries formed "research associations" whose highly specialized libraries conducted a widespread although internal information and publication service in addition to normal library functions. These and other professional libraries of great industrial firms joined in 1924 with associations, institutes, and special libraries interested in technical and industrial literature to form a loose, but workable organization which was named the Association of Special Libraries and Information Bureaux (ASLIB) after the American model.[234] Later general research libraries with their special collections also joined the ASLIB; for they recognized the fact that the new methods of the technological and commercial special libraries could also be applied to special collections in the general sciences. They also realized that problems of acquisition, shelving, indexing, and reference work for professional literature, problems of so-called "documentation," common to all libraries were involved, and these matters occupied a prominent place in discussions at ASLIB meetings.

CHAPTER FIVE

ADMINISTRATIVE AND PROFESSIONAL PROBLEMS

FINANCES AND GROWTH OF COLLECTIONS

Up to the middle of the nineteenth century purchases drawing on funds from stable incomes played a much less important role in acquisition than gifts and endowments. Gifts were not always valuable or desirable acquisitions, and above all a distinct disadvantage was the condition of individual shelving and administration which donors were wont to specify. The holdings of the Bodleian are still composed of 160 separate collections; and ever since Panizzi's day the British Museum has been accustomed to purchase complete collections,[235] a practice which has introduced not only great variety but also much overlapping in the library's structure.[236] In most of the research libraries, as well as in the great municipal libraries, a larger or smaller number of individual collections maintain their special rank and location acquired in either earlier or more recent times. Funds from endowments, subscriptions, fees, or other sources were also generally administered separately and yielded uniformly modest earnings. Even the British Museum received no more than a £900 income from its original foundation endowment around 1850. About the same time the Cambridge University Library could spare only £773 from regular funds for the purchase of books.[237] Oxford had had a similar amount available ever since the beginning of the century, but the other research libraries fell far short of this opulence. Not only acquisition but also administration of libraries were perceptibly hindered by standing committees, commissions, and curators; and the reports of the British Museum commissions and the university commissions contain complaints of the directors against the resultant business difficulties and the restriction of the library's initiative which was indispensable for a successful acquisition policy. A Panizzi could secure necessary freedom of movement by fighting. In 1852 the Cambridge librarian, John Power, exposed before the university commission the administrative disadvantages of a library committee;[238] but even a Bradshaw had to put forward the whole weight of his scholarly reputation to carry out his acquisition policy, which was then fully supported by the university as well.[239]

However, the work of the various commissions did result in larger funds for building up the collection. After 1837 the British Museum was able to increase ordinary expenditures several times and to introduce a policy aimed at the acquisition of every book important for research and every available manuscript without regard to cost. The rising prosperity of the nation and the increasing awareness of the tasks of the British national library provided the requisite means to make desired purchases on all markets until superior American buying power narrowed the field in the seventies. The regular annual appropriations granted to the British Museum by the treasury for book purchases mounted gradually to £6,000. However, the amount remained at this figure, and therefore the Royal Commission on National Museums and Galleries could not refrain from proposing a necessary increase in the book fund in view of the considerably higher prices after World War I. However, it was only in 1930 that as much as £9,000 was appropriated annually for book purchases.[240] The old as well as the new universities have revealed more understanding for building up their collections since the middle of the nineteenth century. The Oxford and Cambridge Act of 1877 attempted to make a better division of total university appropriations[241] by partially diverting the heavy incomes of the colleges to the central libraries. In Oxford ever since the seventies a more rational division of functions between the Bodleian and the college libraries had been discussed time and again, and it had been partially realized by the subordination of a number of libraries to the administration of the Bodleian.[242]

The new universities founded in the seventies and eighties and the academic colleges were basically dependent upon state appropriations from the beginning. When the great philanthropists died off with the Victorian Age, state financing became the rule rather than the exception. For the libraries of the universities and colleges the Universities Grants Committee presents estimates which range from £3,000 to £10,000 and are approved by Parliament according to the customary procedure for granting appropriations.[243]

For a number of older libraries—at present there are six—the copyright privilege is a source of acquisition far more lucrative than the fixed incomes. The older license acts which had been in force since 1662 and the various copyright acts of 1709, 1801, and 1814 had brought valuable as well as minor works into the libraries; but in general the acquisition of copyright titles was so carelessly handled that when the law was revised in 1835 provision was made for the abolition of the privilege for the four Scottish university libraries and for two other libraries.[244] Even in Cambridge, where the law yielded an annual average of 2,983 complete works valued (with other items) at £1,362 during the period 1844-50, the university commission of 1852 requested removal of the privilege.[245] But after Panizzi forced strict observance of the law by his campaign against negligent publishers in 1852,[246] the privilege proved to be a rich source of acquisitions for the British Museum and four other copyright libraries (five after 1911), although the mass of the books flooding the libraries has continually brought up serious problems, above all that of shelving. In Oxford, particularly, opinions have been expressed from time to time demanding strict observance of the scientific character of the library and equally as strict sifting of the material to be kept.[247]

Towards the middle of the century the British Museum with its 435,000 volumes assumed fourth place among the great libraries of Europe, while Oxford, with 220,000, Cambridge, with 167,000, Edinburgh, with 91,000, and Glasgow, with 60,000, stood far behind the largest European libraries, for example, Göttingen, with 360,000 volumes. Annual accessions of the British Museum amounted to some 16,000 volumes.[248] Panizzi estimated that holdings would be doubled in twenty years. In point of fact, the first million was reached during this period, and the second million after about forty years; and within another period of twenty years the holdings were once more doubled, while the rate of acquisition has mounted to over

50,000 volumes annually. Oxford and Cambridge followed in leaps and bounds. Some 3,000,000 and 2,000,000 volumes respectively have been collected by them in the course of the years; and their annual rates of acquisition are about 25,000 and 15,000 volumes respectively. The other research libraries fall in line at some distance behind them.[249] However, the statistics of holdings are not the ultimately decisive factors, but it is rather the nature of the collection and degree of accessibility of the books themselves.

CATALOGING AND CLASSIFICATION

The contributions of Great Britain to the theory of cataloguing and classification are not especially numerous.[250] The systems of Bacon (1605), Bentham (1816), and Coleridge (1818) undertook the classification of human knowledge but not of libraries.[251] The only system drawn up for the classification of books and applied practically during the eighteenth century was that of Conyers Middleton (1755), and this system was restricted in use to Cambridge where it was originated.[252] Of course, English libraries as well as those on the continent have always had systems of shelving. They went back to the medieval custom of arranging books in broad subject groups and within these alphabetically according to author or title. With the growth of book collections and the introduction of stacks arose the necessity of closer classification and transcription of call numbers (British "press-marks") in most alphabetical, printed or manuscript catalogues. Such was the case in Oxford,[253] and it was also undertaken by the British Museum according to a better method devised by Watts, Panizzi, and Winter Jones when the move from the old Montagu House (1838) necessitated a completely new system of shelving. This system was based upon one devised by Thomas Hartwell Horne in 1825.[254] It had seven main classes and numerous subdivisions which in time were increased to 700 and still remain the chief basis of the classification.

Most libraries used some form or another of this type of subject classification up through the nineteenth century. Here and there attempts were made to create philosophically logical or bibliographically practical classifications such as those in the London Library,[255] in the Patent Office Library, in the Cambridge University Library (1845),[256] and in the Glasgow University Library; but on the whole interest for study of classified cataloguing and shelving systems was not very great. In part, this circumstance went together with the fact the subject catalogue as opposed to the alphabetical catalogue had lost a good deal of respect during the discussions of the British Museum catalogue. Dryander's subject catalogue of the Banks collection,[257] much talked of in its day, was equalled by no other work; and after Panizzi it was almost a dogma that the only type of catalogue that could be considered was the alphabetical author catalogue, or at least one with an appended subject index.

The situation changed completely in 1894 when J. D. Brown introduced the "open shelves" system for patrons of the Clerkenwell Public Library. Not only the habits of patrons but also the methods of cataloguing and classification were revolutionized. The necessity of instructing the reader in stack arrangement by a simple, comprehensible classification inspired Brown, together with his co-worker J. H. Quinn, to devise his own method in 1897. In 1897-98 it was improved with his "adjustable classification" and finally replaced in 1906 by a "subject classification."[258] Neither Brown's system nor the one devised by the American, Cutter, about the same time (1891-93)[259] was generally accepted by English libraries, although Brown's open-shelf system and Cutter's dictionary catalogue found the widest acceptance in all Anglo-Saxon public libraries and many research libraries. In the nineties the Dewey decimal classification also became known and adopted in English libraries, not as a method of classified cataloguing but as a system of shelving. Moreover, long before Dewey's day it had been applied in Manchester and Boston (1856) in the form of a stack division by tens.[260] Dewey's decimal system soon made a conquest of British libraries, and it has even been used in the research libraries, for example, Rylands. On the other hand, the Brussels expansion has been adopted only in isolated cases. More recently the Library of Congress system (1909)[261] has won attention if not support. For example, it is used in the National Library of Wales and in the library of the London School of Economics; and the 1927 *Report on Public Libraries in England and Wales*, while recommending Dewey as the best system for public libraries, favored ultimate combination of the two systems.[262]

Aside from the discussions during Panizzi's day, the question of the classified catalogue was revived only in 1897 by Brown and Stanley Jast,[263] who argued that the main catalogue should also be arranged according to the order of the classification. Although English cataloguing theorists have made notable contributions to this problem since that time, and also a few libraries such as the Glasgow Public have published parts of their catalogue in classified form, the classified catalogue as such has been able to make no progress.[264]

The British main catalogue has remained an alphabetical one, either as an author catalogue or as a subject catalogue, and, to a small extent, as a dictionary catalogue. Great Britain can claim the distinction of having created in the famous ninety-one rules for cataloguing in the British Museum the first canon of instructions, thereby laying the foundation on which all later Anglo-American rules have been developed.[265] Even though Panizzi's code was official only for the British Museum, and even though other great libraries, such as the Bodleian and Cambridge University Library, retained their own codes, nevertheless, the British Museum catalogue inspired discussions concerning commonly accepted cataloguing rules. Further impetus was given by Cutter's rules for a dictionary catalogue.[266] A committee appointed by the Library Association worked out proposals which were frequently revised during the years 1879-81 and then accepted as the official code. Upon the instigation of Melvil Dewey the preparation of an Anglo-American code was begun in 1904. By 1908 it had been completed and published.[267]

During the lively discussions before the British Museum Commission the proposal for an English union catalogue appeared frequently, but the struggle to print the British Museum catalogue seemed to be the prerequisite as well as the beginning of the realization of such a project. Soon the idea was publicly discussed. In 1850 Charles Dilke proposed in the *Athenaeum*[268] a catalogue of all books printed before 1600 and in 1877 even wanted to raise the *terminus ante quem* to 1800. Dilke's proposal was expanded by the London Society of Arts in 1878 to a world catalogue to be prepared with international participation.[269] But the conception of a union catalogue (also discussed at the first conference of the Library Association in

1877) was carried to its grave by Richard Garnett when he pointed out to the Library Association in 1892 that the immediate task was the completion of the British Museum catalogue before this Utopian plan could be undertaken.[270]

But no English union catalogue resulted from the completed British Museum catalogue, perhaps because there was no official group prepared to assume the burdens of financing and carrying out the project. Likewise, the British Museum has always been hesitant about cooperative cataloguing projects. The initiative for establishing regional union catalogues lay with the municipal and county libraries; and the first union catalogue was begun in 1931 for the region of the northern counties and all libraries within this area. Other regional union catalogues followed this one, and duplicate entries were sent to the National Central Library in London, thus initiating a national union catalogue which now has over 1,000,000 entries.[271] For the twenty-eight boroughs of London County a union catalogue of non-fiction titles was begun in 1930, and by 1938 it had 1,500,000 cards. The first printed union catalogue was the *World List of Scientific Periodicals* which first appeared in 1925 and again in a second edition in 1931 with almost 24,000 titles. Its counterpart for humanistic disciplines is the *Union List of Periodicals* of 1938, also with about 24,000 titles.[272] However, both of these works approach the line of demarcation between the catalogue and the bibliography.

REGIONALISM AND THE BEGINNINGS OF A NATIONAL LIBRARY SYSTEM[273]

The public library arose and attained its majority as a municipal institution. In the great cities where dozens of libraries did not compete as they did in London, the public library operated as the kernel of a system of service which gradually spread to rural districts and provided for them. But in contrast with the metropolitan districts, the rural regions, i.e., the counties, with their small and medium towns were poorly served by libraries before 1900, indeed, up to World War I. After 1913 the large endowments of Andrew Carnegie furthered the creation of a system of county libraries.[274] A memorandum written in 1915 by Professor Adams of Cambridge for the

Carnegie trustees[275] showed that at that time almost 37 per cent of the total population of 38,000,000 lived in rural districts, but that only 2.5 per cent had access to public or research libraries as opposed to 79 per cent in the cities. The Adams report contributed materially to the passage of the 1931 law by which, among other things, county councils were permitted to establish county libraries. By 1931 the county library system had spread to all the eighty-six counties of Great Britain and the twenty-seven counties of Ireland and was financed by taxation and by grants from Carnegie funds.[276]

Along with many other timely proposals Professor Adams had also urged agreements for interlibrary loans and mutual access which would extend beyond the limits of individual libraries in the city and the country. Such systems, comprising libraries of different administrative status in cities like Manchester, Birmingham, Liverpool, and Glasgow, were realized as a result of this proposal. In 1925 an advisory body was created in London County to straighten out the confused relationships of English libraries and their mutual lending agreements.[277] Two years later the first cooperative association for library activity extending across county lines was created in Cornwall, and it was soon followed by a number of other regional systems. At present there are nine in England and Wales, while in Scotland and Ireland no regular systems have been formed. To date these systems include 479 libraries of all categories which have agreed to make mutual loans. In 1938-39, for example, interlibrary loan figures amounted to 57,135 volumes.[278]

The significant fact about this system of national library cooperation is that not merely municipal and county libraries participate in it but also research libraries, above all university libraries with the exception of libraries of Oxford and Cambridge which do not lend at all. As early as 1923 the Association of University Teachers had urged interlibrary loan between libraries of the universities and the colleges; and in 1925 the Joint Standing Committee on Library Cooperation was founded at the University of Birmingham. It was composed of university instructors and librarians and was connected with an information bureau for the location of desired books.[279] In 1938-39, 7,840 volumes were lent by and to the university libraries.

The various systems of cooperation have found a home office in the National Central Library.[280] Its founding dates back to the Adams report which had proposed the establishment of a Central Library for Students, realized with the aid of the Carnegie trustees. Its original purpose was to form a central depot for books which could not be purchased by most libraries with their limited means and to make this library accessible to scholars and students by a national system of interlibrary loan. Gradually, and with the elimination of none too simple financial and administrative difficulties, the National Central Library was able to increase its income, its holdings, and the number of participating libraries (so-called "outlier libraries") from year to year. The bases of the interlibrary loans were the regional systems and the union catalogue set up by the National Central Library itself. The latter is at once the tool of a national reference department and, more recently, of an international system of interlibrary loan and information exchange extending beyond the limits of Great Britain. After the National Central Library had received a constitution and official recognition with the grant of a Royal Charter in 1931, it was able to move into its new home, the Chaucer House, built with Carnegie funds, in 1933.[281]

BUILDINGS[282]

The beginning of modern library architecture may be fixed in the year 1857 when the famous reading room of the British Museum was opened. It was not only because this circular construction dating back to various plans between 1836 and 1850 and executed by Panizzi in 1852 created an epoch for the genre but even more so because for the first time a clear spatial distinction was made in provisions for use and storage of books.[283] Although the British Museum had had a small reading room since 1757, a larger one since 1774, and a third one since 1838 that was regularly overcrowded, as late as 1850 such a room belonged in no way to the indispensable portions of a library. The Cambridge University Library had no special reading room at all in its old building, which was not vacated until 1934, since nearly all parts of the building were open to patrons.[284] In Oxford the Radcliffe Camera was remodelled as a separate reading room in 1862.[285]

In the Scottish university libraries, just as in the majority of other libraries of Great Britain and Ireland, a kind of "hall library" was predominant throughout the nineteenth century. Books and patrons were accommodated together in a single hall, or in several similar halls where there were annexes. Besides the handsome examples of hall libraries in Trinity College, Cambridge (1695), Trinity College, Dublin (1712-34), Edinburgh University (1823) and elsewhere, this style of architecture had also been used in the Patent Office Library (1855), in the Guildhall Library (1873), in the John Rylands Library (1899), and in many others. The functional construction of a stack room such as the one which surrounded the British Museum's reading room and filled in the open space of the rectangle in Sir Robert Smirke's building not only was the first on English soil but also was far ahead of its time.[286] The circumstances under which the old Montagu House of the British Museum was replaced piecemeal by annexes rather than by a completely new building for lack of space (and money!) have always driven the administration into compromises and forced solutions which in themselves represented brilliant accomplishments but ultimately prevented the British national library from acquiring a modern, complete, and functionally designed building with full provision for future needs.

The library expansion in Oxford must also be discussed as a compromise solution between the tradition-bound Bodleian with its series of reading rooms as a future library center and a functional stack room for the ominously growing collection in the new building on Broad Street.[287] In fact, just as in Cambridge, there was room outside of the medieval city for the construction of a new building; but the magical charm of Duke Humphrey's Library, Arts End, and the Selden Library proved to be stronger than the conception of an unromantic but functional building. The commission set up by the university decided after long study, and then not unanimously, on a solution which provided for the whole problem of book storage in Oxford and at the same time introduced a series of annexes, expansions, and new buildings which was to be concluded with the completion of the new stack building. A comprehensive reorganization of Oxford libraries was undertaken simultaneously. It was to affect catalogues, principles of acquisition, shelving, and use, and even methods of research and instruction. On the other hand, the imposing new University Library in the "Backs" of Cambridge expresses the great importance of this institution by its construction and the old tradition of free access to the stacks in its design; but its location also reveals how the college libraries have remained outside the university library's sphere of influence.[288]

About the turn of the century the other university libraries and many great municipal libraries, like Oxford and Cambridge, suffered from cramped quarters. But it was only after World War I that there came an active period of construction and planning which included all categories of libraries down through the medium-sized towns and villages and in particular the branch libraries of the city systems. In typically British architectural style and with exploitation of experiences of modern American libraries, numerous buildings were erected which were technically sound and, in part, highly representative. The smaller buildings and branch libraries are the only ones which represent any standard type as far as appearance and arrangement are concerned. The large buildings, for example, Cambridge (1934), the central library of Manchester (1934),[289] the Sheffield Public Library (1934),[290] the Leeds University Library (1936),[291] the National Library of Wales (1937),[292] the plans for the university libraries of Liverpool (1936), Manchester (1937), London (1937),[293] of the National Library of Scotland (1937),[294] and of the University College in London (1937),[295] all represent thoroughly individualistic solutions of very different types of problems. If one compares the rectangular library of Aberystwyth (begun in 1911) with its inner courts and the compact central library of Manchester with its more intellectual than practical construction, or the London University Library with its tower reminiscent of American models, a rich variety of planning and execution is apparent.

Nevertheless, common traits peculiar to modern British architectural trends are not lacking. With the exception of Oxford, it can hardly be said that there has been an attempt to plan for future developments not discernible at present for more than about two or three generations to come. The possibility of expansion has been anticipated generally; and only in Manchester, with its complete, circular construction and room for 1,500,000 volumes, has an upper limit been set (by the dome), however generous it may be. The modern principle of utmost exploitation of space has been followed, in part with the sacrifice of light in the interior or underground locations of the stacks in Manchester, Oxford, Liverpool and elsewhere. Most librarians and architects agree with Jast, who conceived the Manchester building, that horizontal extension of the stack is preferable to vertical.[296] Neither has the design of the stack as a web been developed so consistently anywhere as it has been in Manchester. In the new Oxford building the stack section, like the annexes of the Library of Congress, is surrounded on all four sides by exits from reading rooms and staff quarters. As a result of frequent multiplicity of special and separately shelved collections in one and the same building, the construction of independent complexes of rooms with their own reading rooms and stacks came to the forefront. Examples are the London School of Economics and the University College,[297] but in no case have so many divisions been established as in numerous American libraries. Likewise, in the rooms open to the public, in the vestibules, staircases, and reading rooms there has been a general disinclination toward all decoration without sacrificing legitimate dignity. On the whole, recent British library architecture has perhaps brought no fundamental progress but has equated inherited principles with modern exigencies.

THE LIBRARY PROFESSION

The English librarian enters into the full light of historical dignity in the person of Thomas James, Bodley's librarian. Through the centuries he was succeeded by a long line of remarkable personalities, many of whom were distinguished as scholars. Were they the only bearers of the torch of library history? In reply, one might almost say that more notice might be given the libraries' founders than their administrators. It was only with Panizzi that the librarian appears as a formative and dominating force, for he developed the laws of administration and use and turned museum collections into functional institutions. It was only after the library was recognized as a public institution which required trained workers that a professional conscience of librarianship could arise. That it was condi-

tioned by the age may be seen from the fact that the library movement in Great Britain and the United States came forward at the
same time. Priority was denied the mother country; but in the year
after the Philadelphia convention of 1876 the first international congress was held in London, and the Library Association of the United
Kingdom was founded.[298]

The British professional association is much closer to the American than any other European group in respect to organization and
purposes. Just as in the case of most British corporation articles, those
of the Library Association drawn up on October 5, 1877, and the
Royal Charter of 1898 confirming them,[299] were based on the idea of
self-rule and the inclusion of all persons interested in the library
profession. Accordingly, not only librarians but also members of
library committees and functionaries of local governments and other
corporate bodies belonged to the Library Association. Although this
situation made the formation of a sharply defined profession of librarianship difficult, there was the advantage of winning public
attention from a broader foundation and influence in the distribution of public funds. The English librarian has become a master of
the fine art of injecting his personality into the board of trustees or
the library committee, thereby directing the course of events in the
interest of his institution. On the other hand, it is not to be overlooked that the heterogeneous elements represented in the Library
Association have often caused friction, and the standpoints of local
politics, for example in matters of appointments and salaries, are
put ahead of material considerations. The generally dominant influence of library authorities has also had the consequence that
within the Library Association the public libraries have influenced
collective policies out of proportion to their own significance.

The conditions of the Victorian period favored rapid growth of
the Library Association.[300] When local and regional groups were
formed after the eighties, branch and provincial associations were
organized, while groups of assistants, university and special librarians
founded sections to provide for their special needs. Soon after the
semicentennial conference of Edinburgh the membership had grown
to 4,000, and the volume of business was so great that permanent
headquarters were established in 1933 in the Chaucer House.

At the founding convention it was decided to use the American *Library Journal* as the temporary organ of the British association, but this plan was given up in 1882 as impractical. From 1879 to 1885 the conferences published *Transactions and Proceedings,* from 1880 to 1888 the *Library Chronicle,* and from 1889 to 1898 *The Library* attempted to reflect the interests of the association; but permanent success was attained only in 1899 with the founding of the *Library Association Record.* The unorthodox, often dissident *Library Assistant* has appeared as the organ of younger librarians since 1898. An important part of the work of the association and the committees has appeared in the official and semiofficial reports of committees established for consideration of special questions. The 1927 *Report on Public Libraries in Great Britain and Ireland,* written by librarians and educators at the request of the Board of Education, used the Adams report as a point of departure. It was supplemented by an addendum of 1927 and a *Survey of Libraries* during the period 1936-37, and still today it is the basis for discussion of the most important problems of public libraries.[301] The problems of the state and university libraries have been handled in their respective reports. All these reports of committees are mines of information for British library history, not infrequently going further into the realm of general library history. James Duff Brown's *Handbook of Library Appliances* (1892) signalled the beginning of a series of monographs and bibliographies,[302] among which the *Subject Index to Periodicals* (1915 to date) and the *Year's Work in Librarianship* (1929 to date) deserve special mention. Since 1892 the Library Association has also published an official *Yearbook.*

The relatively slow adoption of library laws and the unsatisfactory financial situation of research as well as public libraries has again and again directed the attention of the Library Association and also of the public to a weak spot of British librarianship, viz., the uncertainty of the library profession, the absence of binding regulations for admission and education, and the resulting disproportionate, indeed, unworthy economic and social position of librarians which brought about a certain contempt for the cultural and social accomplishments of the library itself.[303] To change this situation was one of the foremost purposes of the Library Association.[304] As early as 1880-82 plans for training assistants were worked out, and the first professional examination was held in 1885. The Royal Charter of 1898 gave the Library Association express permission to hold examinations and grant certificates. However, the results of the regulations of 1891-1907 were hardly satisfactory, above all because admission was not dependent upon certification of minimum educational attainments. After 1904 at least certification of practical experience in library work was required; but only in 1924 was university matriculation set forth as a prerequisite of admission.

An important step on the road to uniform training was the establishment of courses of academic instruction by the education committee of the Library Association and the London School of Economics. This led in 1919 to the founding of the School of Librarianship at the University College in London.[305] Its expenses were borne chiefly by the Carnegie Trust. The two-year courses end with elementary, intermediate, and final examinations and a diploma from the school, which, however, is no guarantee of a position. Significantly, the large state and university libraries in general have trained their assistants under their own roofs. Likewise the local governments showed little inclination to consider diplomas from the library school or the Library Association in filling positions (and paying salaries!). However, the *Report on Public Libraries in Great Britain and Ireland* correctly points out that public administrators must be educated to demanding only trained and approved librarians.[306] Still a satisfactory solution of all professional questions may be reached only when the government approaches more firmly than before its task of establishing central regulation, supervision, and financing of libraries throughout the entire country.

CONCLUSION

This outline of British library history can only attempt to point up certain outstanding lines and tendencies of new developments. Details, names, and events must be forced into the background or omitted altogether. But perhaps the survey will reveal that there has hardly been uniform development of a national form of librarianship and that modern developments really started only with Panizzi, and British librarianship only with the founding of the Library Association and the public library movement. Fundamentally, however, England, Scotland, Ireland, and even Wales, have their own library history so that the story as a whole is broken up into details, held together, to be sure, by common traits of Anglo-Saxon character. One of them is the strong, frequently decisive influence of the private collector and his highly developed sense of responsibility to his country. The development and success of the most important libraries should be ascribed to this circumstance. But while the regular transition of private collections into public ownership strengthened state libraries, it did not mean an end of private initiative.

In addition to private collectors there was the independent work of corporations, communities, and patrons, with the state remaining in the background up to the present time and exercising its cultural and political influence more by administration and appropriation than by laws and regulations. As an organ of self-government and as a legal corporation the Library Association exercises a definitive influence on the nature of library work and the expansion of the field in general. The library movement as shaped by the Library Association has created norms for the movement and furthered its recognition. A uniform type of British librarian will hardly emerge in

79

the classical land of individualism, just as in the past the development of the most important libraries was determined for long periods by the personalities of their directors. Nevertheless, individualism at present is being heavily counterbalanced by the modern movement of regional and national cooperation promoted by the state.

Part II

THE UNITED STATES OF AMERICA

INTRODUCTION [307]

Including the colonial period, the national development of the United States is crowded into a period of only three centuries. The rise of the American nation and the American people took place, as it were, before a world-wide public, and, unique in the history of mankind, the chronicle of this tumultuous development was preserved from the very beginning in documents, tracts, and books. At the threshold of colonial history stands the *True Relation of Occurences and Accidents*[308] which the founder of the oldest colony published in 1608. The Pilgrim fathers took with them in books that part of the wisdom and thought of their old home which seemed good and salutary to them. Political, social, and cultural ideas and the scientific thought of Europe forced their way into the young American state with books. Books accompanied the pioneers of the nineteenth century on their treks over the great rivers and savannas, and they bore the concepts of civilization and culture into the mountain valleys of Oregon and the gold mining towns of California. Books were sources of knowledge before there were schools, and collections of books and libraries competed with schools in education and culture. Books provided knowledge, learning, and skill; they helped in the struggle for existence, helped settle and conquer the land; but they also helped to beautify and deepen life. From the earliest days the American people were convinced that books and reading could lead to a progressive improvement of man and of political and social institutions; and thus libraries as well have gradually attained recognition in the eyes of the American people. America and her libraries have grown without the onus or blessing of tradition. The way has at times been stormy, not always free from error, but success has been won in many fields where older nations failed.[309]

CHAPTER SIX

THE COLONIAL PERIOD

GENERAL SURVEY; COLLEGE LIBRARIES

The entire seventeenth and first half of the eighteenth century produced neither educational institutions nor libraries of any great importance. Nevertheless, there was a remarkable difference between the cultural orientation of the New England colonies and the regions south of the Chesapeake Bay. Virginia, Maryland, the Carolinas, and Georgia represented the aristocratic elements well into the nineteenth century. The dominant planting and land-owning families of English descent held to English traditions and culture. They were accustomed to send their sons to be educated in England if they did not hire tutors to do the job at home. There was scarcely any inclination to establish schools of higher or lower grade.[310] Old Cantabrigians in Virginia attempted to establish a college in 1622; but William and Mary College was not founded until 1693, and its library was totally insignificant until well into the nineteenth century.[311] Although during the eighteenth century the Southern colonies enjoyed considerable immigration of Irish, Scottish, French, and especially Palatinate refugees who brought a certain element of culture and intellectual demands with them, no higher institutions were established, not to mention libraries. Perhaps it was because "the past represented simply a state of things from which they had escaped, and for which they had neither regrets nor respectful memories."[312]

Likewise, the Puritans, Presbyterians, and Independents, who had been forced to leave their homes on account of religious persecution by the High Anglican Church and who had settled in Massachusetts and the northern sections, had no intention of carrying England with

84

them but rather of creating something which was not England. And the Quakers, the Dutch and German Mennonites who colonized the Hudson Valley and Pennsylvania in the seventeenth century must have had a similar purpose in mind. Nevertheless, cultural, social, and political life here followed a totally different course than it did in the South; for the austere puritanism and sectarianism, which found the meaning and purpose of life in the fulfillment of religious and civil duties, were not satisfied with reading the Bible and didactic tracts but also valued the educational merits of history, philosophy, the classics, and even belles-lettres. It is no accident that education and science found their first permanent seats in the northern colonies.

Even among the Pilgrim fathers and the immigrants of the first decades there had been remarkably many personalities of education and learning, most of them Cantabrigians from Trinity and Emanuel Colleges.[313] Among the latter was John Harvard, from whose legacy of 1638 the first college on American soil and the first library of 380 volumes were founded. The fact that Harvard soon became the first school of puritanism[314] must be ascribed to the influence of the Mather dynasty of theologians.[315] Theology was the principal course of instruction; and theological and didactic literature represented the better part of the library, which, according to Cotton Mather, was the best in the country about 1700 but still far removed from the Bodleian or the Vatican. Even after a fire of 1764 had destroyed almost the entire library of 5,000 volumes and a new one was established from endowments, theological literature, as revealed by the catalogue of 1790,[316] was again in the foreground. But after the fire, in the wake of the revived interest for classics, science, history, politics, law, and English literature, the chief works in these disciplines found a place in Harvard Hall.

Like Harvard, the eight other colleges of the colonial period were also primarily theological schools, in which, however, statesmen, judges, physicians, and scholars were also educated, a fact reflected in the book lists of the weak libraries. Towards the end of the eighteenth century there were some 13,000 volumes in Harvard, 4,000 in Yale, and 3,000 in Dartmouth. Only a few of these early libraries were able to tide their holdings over the Revolution, and most of them suffered heavily from fire and plunder.[317]

PRINTING; PRIVATE AND SEMIPUBLIC COLLECTIONS

One year after the founding of Harvard the first printing press on American soil was established in Cambridge. It existed for fifty years and exercised an obvious influence on the intellectual life of the Massachusetts Colony.[318] By 1680 there were nine presses in Boston, and under the influence of the Quakers a printing house was opened in Philadelphia in 1688, the same year in which Virginia made the first feeble but abortive attempt to operate a press. In the Southern colonies printing houses were not permitted until 1730, and up to the end of the colonial period there were no more than nineteen presses altogether on American soil. Theology led their productions with a quota of 33 per cent. Book publishing was insignificant in comparison with book imports from the mother country and other European lands. For, in spite of growing political independence, the New Englanders as well as the Southerners laid great weight on the continuation of relations with the home country and its book trade. The family library of the Mathers, which numbered 4,000 volumes at the beginning of the eighteenth century, was composed largely of European works; and the family library of Governor Winthrop was built up from English and French trade lists and the catalogues of German fairs.

Ownership of a private library corresponded to the inner inclinations and tastes of the age in the educated circles of the cultural North as well as in the rich families of the South.[319] Collections of 3,000 or 4,000 volumes were not infrequent; and not only the best older and contemporary authors of Europe but also many older American works, passed over by the colleges, found their way to these libraries.[320] Even in the nineteenth century visitors in Southern plantation homes could marvel at the rare libraries brought together in cosmopolitan taste. But most of those spared by the Revolution were sacrificed to the senseless ravages of the War Between the States.

Many of these older private collections have passed into public ownership by legacy or assumed a public character in the lifetimes of their owners. But the conception of a public library was still unknown in the seventeenth century. Even though the city of Boston already had small collections under the designation of Publick Library toward the middle and last quarter of the century, they were actually foundations for the benefit of clergymen and educated laymen.[321] The municipalities still felt far removed from the responsibility of providing reading matter. In 1647 the colony of Massachusetts passed a law by which the communities were bound to establish schools, even though the primary objective was to combat more effectively the malevolence of Satan.[322] In New England and Pennsylvania community schools spread very rapidly, and with them the number of literate persons in need of cultural opportunities.

Matters progressed more slowly in the Southern colonies. About the turn of the century the latter received small and publicly accessible book collections, thanks to the labors of the English clergyman Dr. Thomas Bray, who set for himself the task of establishing parish libraries in the British plantations. Bray personally founded some thirty such libraries in Maryland and, shortly after 1700, even "Lending Laymen's Libraries," individual remnants of which later passed into public libraries.[323]

The Eighteenth Century; Franklin; Society Libraries

However, these efforts were without permanent effects. The decisive step towards the development of a public library system was taken in 1731 when Benjamin Franklin, who himself had experienced the blessing of books in his youth of toil, founded, together with a few friends, the Library Company,[324] the ancestor of all North American lending libraries. The small but rapidly growing library was dependent upon voluntary contributions of members, and it was to serve the cultural needs of workmen, skilled laborers, and merchants. Franklin felt that the time was ripe for supplementing the parochial school bound in puritanic tradition with a new, higher medium of education and for revealing to the people the way to intellectual culture through the arts and sciences. Franklin's foundation was the first step toward democratization of education and libraries,[325] and it served as a model far and wide. In 1745 James Logan of Philadelphia left his significant library for similar purposes.[326] In Charleston, where metropolitan culture had already developed in the seventeenth century, the first and only public library in the South was founded in 1748 on a subscription basis.

In a number of New England cities reading and discussion groups were formed in the following decades. They were ordinarily connected with libraries [327] and enjoyed great popularity among the broad masses of the population. In addition, educational and forensic associations and the philosophical societies, the first of which was organized by Franklin in 1743 in Philadelphia, came into existence during the latter part of the eighteenth century. Their libraries reached pretentious stages at an early date, and they collected publications of learned societies from home and abroad. The nineteenth century was the golden age for these societies, comparable in some respects to contemporary German and English philosophical and scientific societies.

Of the many attempts to create a system of public libaries, relatively few survived the stormy period of the Revolution. Nevertheless, there were some fifty such libraries with about 80,000 volumes towards the end of the eighteenth century. The heritage left by the thirteen colonies to the young independent nation was not significant in extent. The most valuable gain was perhaps the conception of a society library based on subscription, the idea on which the later public library was based. American libraries still lacked immediate contact with European science and libraries, and it was only with the dawn of the nineteenth century that European thought and expression began to be received.

CHAPTER SEVEN

FROM 1789 TO 1875

GENERAL SURVEY

The solemn announcement of the Constitution in 1787 in no way meant the beginning of orderly national life. The violent ideological clashes between Federalists and Unionists, later between Democrats and Republicans, accompanied political developments through almost the entire nineteenth century and developed into numerous crises. But they also enriched political and intellectual life and called forth a valuable literature at an early date. The citizens of the young republic followed the speeches and publications of the political and intellectual leaders of the nation with greatest interest,[328] and the ideas and literature of the French Revolution were received enthusiastically. The great events before and after the turn of the century inspired historical literature on both the immediate and more distant past. Historical societies especially devoted to local history came into existence. The nascent national conscience called forth a powerful, autochthonous American literature. One of the most important generations of historians, politicians, and legal scholars was lined up beside a generation of naturalists, travellers, and explorers.

But the intellectual contribution of this inspired era found no state or public libraries prepared to receive and preserve their work, and it was collected rather by a few individual connoisseurs, academies, athenaea, and other institutions. Surveying the library history of the nineteenth century, one sees a development which differs in all its basic traits from the German and European, excepting perhaps the English. Whereas in Continental Europe it was felt that the leadership and cooperation of the state was almost a matter of course, this idea was almost completely absent in the United States. This circumstance is partially explained by the federal Constitution which, according to article I, section 8, gives Congress power "to promote the progress of science and the useful arts"[329] but makes no statement about public education, not to mention libraries. Cultural matters were left to the care of the several states which, in their turn, according to the old English administrative practice, delegated their powers to local authorities, county and municipal. The first half of the century passed before the municipalities, inspired by state laws, gave their attention to libraries. And the federal government, which only half-heartedly promoted the growth of the Library of Congress and a few bureau libraries, did not enter the scene of American librarianship until 1876 when it published a basic official document.[330] Up to this time it was scarcely possible to speak of a scientific national librarianship, even in the colleges and universities.

Provision for scholarly institutions was ordinarily left to the initiative of private individuals or groups; and even in the late nineteenth century the American millionaire still assumed functions which in Europe fell into the sphere of the state. The entire period from 1800 to 1875 is full of the entrepreneur spirit in all aspects of political, industrial, and cultural life. The general prosperity surely benefited the libraries, but the driving force was self-help. It was only after the middle of the century that legislation came to the aid of libraries and guided developments into a new path.

SUBSCRIPTION, PROPRIETARY, AND SCHOOL-DISTRICT LIBRARIES

The need for reading and the struggles for culture during the second half of the eighteenth century had brought forth plans for subscription and proprietary libraries. With the dawn of a new age they took on new tasks and new life. Inasmuch as the university libraries failed to function properly, the subscription and proprietary libraries attracted a large proportion of learned activities; and since they were usually connected with academies, museums, and philosophical and scientific societies, they inclined after a fashion to become scholarly libraries. Dependent upon shares, endowments, and legacies from their wealthiest members, they were also in a position to purchase good and even expensive books, to print their own publications, and to exchange publications with foreign societies. Such relationships were extensively promoted by the trips of American laymen and scholars to European countries as early as the first decades of the nineteenth century, frequently undertaken with the secondary motive of purchasing books.

The most prominent example of this type of library was the magnificent collection of the Boston Athenaeum, which was founded in 1807 and gradually increased its general and special holdings for the enrichment of Boston's intellectual life throughout the entire century.[331] This library, like its sister institutions in Philadelphia, New York, and numerous other cities, is thoroughly comparable with the best English and Continental society libraries in size, external appearance, and service. The golden age of the society libraries lasted through the final quarter of the century; and some have preserved their independence, although most of them were associated with the great municipal libraries or completely amalgamated with them, just as in the case of most European society libraries.

While these libraries appealed to a fairly limited circle of scholars and wealthy men, there was no lack of institutions which provided for cultural needs of the great city masses, workmen, mechanics, merchants, and skilled laborers. The technological age which dawned in the 1820's,[332] the beginning of industrial expansion, trade, and communications put forward demands which could only be satisfied by special knowledge and skills. The public schools were still in their first stages, and trade schools were almost nonexistent. Accordingly, the mechanics' institutes[333] were founded as self-supporting institutions by the people who were dependent upon industry. Lectures and courses were given and with a revival of Franklin's ideas, lending libraries for the members were connected with them. These mechanics' institutes played a significant role, and some of them have been changed into polytechnical institutes while others have persisted as such until the present day.

Closely related to them were the apprentices' libraries, the first of which was founded in Philadelphia in 1820. Individual mechanics' and apprentices' libraries reached the point of 20,000 volumes and more. Still more significant were the mercantile libraries,[334] which likewise arose after 1820 and might perhaps be compared with the

German mercantile and trade organizations, although they were also social in character and followed an educational policy formulated for benefit of the merchants' successors. In part the statistics of their holdings were quite considerable. Individual ones had more than 50,000 volumes around 1875, and those of New York and Philadelphia, even had 160,000 and 125,000 volumes respectively.

If the typical American notion that books and libraries were among the bases of education and culture was revealed in these early institutions, then the close connection between school and library in America appeared all the more impressive in the school-district libraries. The school laws[335] of New York State passed in 1812 and 1827 had recommended the establishment of libraries which were to be available to pupils and teachers alike; and by a law of 1835 the levying of taxes for these purposes by administrative units of school districts was approved. The success was enormous. By 1850, 8,000 libraries with 1,300,000 volumes altogether had arisen in some 11,000 school districts, which, however, were often rather small in extent. In Massachusetts, where the school system had been organized by the great educator Horace Mann, there were some 700 libraries open to the public by 1850. By 1876 seventeen more states had also introduced this system. Even though it enjoyed no permanence because of the weakness of the school districts, and even though the existing libraries were turned into purely school libraries toward the end of the century, the system was important as a forerunner of the public libraries.[336]

FREE PUBLIC LIBRARIES

The exclusive subscription and proprietary libraries could no longer satisfy the reading needs of the metropolitan population toward the middle of the century. If the book was to serve as a cultural medium, then it must also be made freely available to the poorer classes. The prerequisites for the creation of an effective public library were present: Franklin had already thought out the idea of a public library; the school libraries had proved the cultural value of books; the social libraries had spread ideas about the common usefulness of libraries; and the school legislation had shown the communities the way by which they could help themselves secure the means for cultural institutions. But, in point of fact, a few New England cities had granted appropriations by ordinance for the establishment and support of libraries even before 1850.

However, the decisive step was taken by the first literary city of the nation, Boston, when on March 18, 1848, it passed a special law permitting the establishment of a public library and the levying of an annual tax up to $5,000 for its support.[337] The plans which had been making the public rounds for ten years previously could now be realized, and within a short time money and books were collected from subscription and endowment. The city[338] selected from municipal officials and the citizenry a board of trustees which was the legal owner of library property and was to operate as a competent supervisory body. In March 1854 the Free Public Library was opened under a Massachusetts statute, the world's first library law.[339] Regulations for its use were remarkably modern: The reading room was open to all adults without formalities and to young people with recommendations, and lending was dependent upon conditions which were easy to satisfy. In Charles Coffin Jewett[340] the library received in 1857 its first important director, and he was followed by the equally significant Justin Winsor (1868-77),[341] both of them personalities who deserve a place in history as cofounders of modern American librarianship.

But the moving spirit in the establishment of the library committee was George Ticknor,[342] who had learned to appreciate the advantages of the great German libraries during his European travels and had come home convinced that a great public library could be the culmination of an educational system and the best means of enabling the people to formulate their political ideas independently.[343] Therefore he put great emphasis on the value of popular literature and a free lending policy, whereas other influential personalities such as the Harvard professor Edward Everett[344] represented the conception of the educated classes that a public library should be an institution for general research and not a lending library. Had Everett's ideas been accepted, the free public libraries would probably have been pushed into the background by municipal research libraries. Nevertheless, the brilliant development of a new type of library in

Boston as well as in other cities has justified Ticknor's ideas.

Ticknor agreed with Everett and others in the concept that the public municipal library should also serve the serious scholar. After the Free Lending Library was assured, he successfully urged the creation of a research division, the Reference Library. A few years earlier in 1848 the Astor family library, the first scholarly private collection in the country, had passed into municipal ownership in New York.[345] It was the kernel of the New York Public Library which was not established until a later consolidation of several other libraries, and its example and success promoted the formation of central municipal libraries in other cities. Since the latter ordinarily had a non-lending reference division side by side with the lending division, a highly significant new type of library was created for the American public library system, thereby preventing a separation of the popular from the scholarly orientation. And here too is the basis for the circumstance that the free public library could assume in the life of the American city a totally different position from that of the German *Stadtbibliothek* of the second half of the nineteenth century, and, further, that the public libraries played a role in national cultural life distinct from that of the German popular library.

The Boston library law was extended in 1851 to include the whole state of Massachusetts;[346] and by 1875, 144 communities had made use of the permission to levy taxes for library purposes. During the following decades most states followed suit with the same or similar legislation. Between 1850 and 1875, 257 free public libraries in all were founded, a figure which was, however, rather modest by comparison with the grand total of 2,240 new libraries established during this period.[347] However, by 1875 there was no longer any doubt that the future belonged to the public library.

The state libraries did not actually belong among public libraries in the beginning. The first one was founded in 1811 in New Jersey, and one state after another followed in establishing these libraries in the capital cities for official and legislative purposes.[348] By 1850 thirty states had them, and by 1875 all states had libraries ranging from 10,000 to 40,000 volumes.[349] Consistent with their purposes, they collected chiefly the literature of administration, legislation, and jurisprudence, but soon they also extended their field to local history, newspapers, and general literature.[350] An early system of mutual exchange of documents had been extended to all states by 1875, although an attempt to assure depository copies of federal publications to all of them failed. Even though these libraries were only designed for local use and not for lending, they were open not merely to state officials but also to the local citizens and all serious users. Since, in addition, the state capitols were nearly always located in a small city in which there was usually no other public library, the state libraries gradually assumed the function of the latter. It was also an easy step for them to assume a position as the center of use and advisory service for surrounding rural districts. When, in the last quarter of the century, all states established library commissions to provide for the counties and funds for county libraries, the state libraries assumed the job of central administration and direction.

Research Libraries

In 1800 there were scarcely a dozen libraries which deserved the name of a research library. During the first half of the century the libraries of the colleges and universities were unable to attract research workers, the sole exception being Harvard whose library contained about 25,000 volumes in 1850. However, that was not even a fifth of the number that Göttingen could boast; and the libraries of Yale, Princeton, and the other colleges were far behind Harvard. Scholars had to go abroad if they wanted to write their books from original sources, and even in 1848 Charles Jewett, at that time librarian of the Smithsonian Institution, could point to a number of American books written in Europe for which the literature necessary to their composition was largely absent from American libraries.[351]

The lacunae in the nation's collections of books had long been the subject of public complaint. Perhaps they were felt nowhere more keenly than in Washington where the best minds of the land had gathered for the Congress. The first two presidents, Washington and Adams, were connoisseurs and collectors of books, and the third, Jefferson, used his personal influence to put the collections of both houses together as the Library of Congress (1802).[352] When it was destroyed by the English in 1812 it contained 3,000 volumes. The attempt at that time to compare this deed with the destruction of the library at Alexandria gave entirely too much honor to the Library of Congress, but the event was felt as a national loss. In 1815 Congress purchased Jefferson's private collection of 6,400 volumes as the basis of a new library; and it appropriated occasional funds as well as an annual grant of $5,000 (after 1824) for the acquisition of standard European works. Congress also gave it depository rights for all American official documents and the legal publications of the individual states, but it was unable to comprehend the idea of a national library. Although the first librarian, George Watterson (1815-29), received powerful support from the library committee which had been in existence since 1805,[353] he could not convince Congress of the necessity of transforming an official library into a universal national library.

Because of Congress' parsimonious attitude the opportunity to purchase large, complete collections on the European market was not used. American private collectors and above all the British Museum won a headstart not to be overtaken in the race to collect early American literature. Likewise, the international exchange system introduced in 1839 by the Frenchman Alexandre Vattemare with the approval of Congress brought many valuable official French documents, but in 1859 it was permitted to lapse.[354] After the acquisition of the Smithsonian Collection in 1846 a unique opportunity for the creation of a national library was presented. The imposing sum afforded by the endowment permitted Jewett to build up a collection of society publications, bibliographies, and catalogues unrivalled at the time. According to Jewett's plan the Smithsonian Library was to have depository rights on all American imprints, and it was to do central cataloguing and publish an American national bibliography.[355] Jewett and the library committee feverishly defended the case for a national library before Congress and the public; but Congress killed these plans in 1854, Jewett was forced to resign, and hopes for an American national library had to be put aside for several decades. The devastating fire which broke out in the Library of Congress on December 24, 1851 and destroyed 35,000 out of 55,000 volumes also placed a temporary hindrance on its development.

The Origins of Special Libraries

On his trip through the United States Friedrich von Raumer[356] found that although no collections of books were comparable to the great European libraries, many libraries had been founded for and were industriously used by lawyers, physicians, clergymen, merchants, and others in the larger cities of the East. For the practical purpose of technical and mercantile affairs there had been special libraries since the 1820's, and in point of fact it was at this time that the first special technological libraries appeared.[357] In this category must also be listed the libraries of the historical societies which arose toward the beginning of the nineteenth century and successfully gathered the sources and the printed materials on local history. Likewise, there were the often very significant collections of the hospitals and of the medical, scientific, and philosophical societies and academies. Originally state libraries also were a type of special library in that they served governmental agencies primarily.

Bureau libraries had been founded in Washington for official purposes as early as the first half of the nineteenth century and particularly in the sixties. Of these the Patent Office (1839), the Department of Agriculture (1860), and the Surgeon General's Office developed purely special libraries of national importance.[358] Likewise there was a tendency to form special collections in the great universities designed to train men for such definite professions as law, theology, and medicine. The library of the Harvard Law School, still today the most important legal library in the country, was founded in 1817; and one of the best medical libraries, that of the College of Physicians in Philadelphia, even goes back to the eighteenth century (1789). The golden age of special libraries was about the turn of the century, but the notion of a scholarly research library received definitive form in these early forerunners sooner than in any European nation.

CHAPTER EIGHT

FROM 1876 TO THE PRESENT

GENERAL SURVEY

The centennial of American independence fell in a period of incredible economic prosperity for the United States. The destruction of the War Between the States had its effects well into the Era of Corruption, but it was soon overcome by the healthy forces of economic retrenchment. The territorial, economic, and industrial expansion revealed unlimited possibilities. The population of scarcely 40,000,000 in 1876 reached 75,000,000 by 1900. The great American fortunes were established; and the wealth of the nation was expressed not only in factories, highways, and railroads, but also in imposing monuments of culture, schools, museums, and libraries.

The library profession as well enjoyed a period of boundless prosperity in the last quarter of the century; and it seemed all the more astounding because the external development prior to 1876 had been none too brilliant. Nevertheless, this year witnessed two events which revealed the powerful inner vitality of the libraries: the founding of the American Library Association and the publication of the Bureau of Education's report on the libraries of the nation. This report was not only the first official survey of American librarianship as a whole but also announced publicly and emphatically the participation of the federal government in library work, which was recognized as an educational force alongside the schools of the nation.

GERMAN INFLUENCES ON AMERICAN SCHOLARSHIP AND RESEARCH LIBRARIES

Development and organization of the academic and specialized

98

research libraries now kept closer pace with the progress of American scientific thought and method than during the first half of the century. But the latter were completely under the influence of German thought and German literature.[359] German idealism and transcendentalism, classical and romantic poetry, the writings of Schleiermacher and of German theologians forced their way into the American universities and their libraries. The University of Virginia introduced German into its curriculum in 1825, and Harvard College followed suit in 1830. After 1867 the philosophy of Kant and Hegel was revealed to broader circles. These influences were intensified by the activity of numerous university teachers who, like Everett and Ticknor in an earlier period, had studied in the German universities and learned their methods of instruction. Henry Tappan, first president of the University of Michigan, recommended in his book of 1851 on university education the Prussian system as the glorious accomplishment of an enlightened and energetic despotism and as the most perfect in the world.[360] In these decades Germany won laurels as the nation of academic freedom, and American youth considered it an honor to earn a German academic degree.

But even more important were the immediate influences. After 1871 the lecture and seminar method was adopted at Michigan and later at other colleges inspired by German models. In 1873 Harvard introduced the German Ph.D. and Michigan followed suit in 1876. In the same year Johns Hopkins University in Baltimore was established precisely after German style with no college curriculum, only postgraduate work. Together with these decisive innovations the spirit of German instructional and research methods forced its way into many American universities and colleges; and even though the typical American textbook method with its hidebound pedantic process of listening and reciting could not be abolished, the way was at least opened up for independent selection of books and research from original sources. These circumstances quite naturally had a favorable effect on the policy of acquisition and position of libraries within the organism of the university. These movements were consciously promoted by such important university presidents as Charles K. Adams of Michigan, Cornell, and Wisconsin, Daniel Coit Gilman of Hopkins and Charles W. Eliot of Harvard.[361]

German influences on the scholarly life of America were soon reflected in the holdings of American libraries. There was a heavy demand for German books, manuscripts, and private and scholarly libraries. American collectors or their agents appeared in European markets, and the prices they offered started a migration of book collections to the new world. One of the first, the library of Christian Daniel Ebeling (died 1817)[362] with thousands of American maps and rare newspapers of the eighteenth and early nineteenth centuries, was bought for Harvard College. A few years later, in 1824, the theological books and parts of the great manuscript collection of Professor Leander van Ess of Darmstadt[363] went overseas, and more important collections of German theologians followed in the next decades: In 1856 the 4,000 volume collection of the New Testament scholar Georg Christian Lücke of Göttingen; in 1866 the 7,000 volumes of the ecclesiastical historian C. W. Niedner of Berlin; and shortly thereafter the collections of the ecclesiastical historian August Neander (died 1850) and the Berlin dogmatist E. W. Hengstenberg (died 1869).[364]

In the last third of the century American interest was especially directed toward Germanic and philological collections. The libraries of Franz Bopp (died 1867), J. Bernays (died 1881), Wilhelm Scherer (died 1886), F. A. Pott (died 1887), R. Bechstein (died 1894) and Friedrich Zarncke (died 1891) were acquired by American universities.[365] Regretfully but according to the wishes of her husband the widow of Paul de Lagarde sold his library of 5,000 volumes to the New York University, only to be able to turn over the 30,000 marks it brought to the Paul de Lagarde Stiftung. Around the turn of the century the library of the Germanic scholar Matthias Lexer (died 1892), the 10,000 volumes of Rudolf Hildebrand, and the 7,200 volumes of Richard Heinzel (died 1905) went the same way.[366] The libraries of Hermann Sauppe (died 1893), Heinrich von Brunn (died 1894), Martin Hertz (died 1895), Otto Ribbeck (died 1898), and the 7,000 volumes of Kurt Wachsmuth (died 1905)[367] yielded rich acquisitions for classical philology and archaeology.

Likewise the golden era of German political, legal, and historical scholarship has made its contribution to the growth of American libraries. The rich collections of Robert von Mohl (died 1875) and

Ernst Curtius (died 1896) were acquired by Yale. The important libraries of G. L. von Maurer (died 1872) and Konrad von Maurer (died 1904) went to Harvard. The books of J. K. Bluntschli (died 1881) found a permanent home at Johns Hopkins, and the extensive collections of Leopold von Ranke (died 1886) are preserved at Syracuse as a special unit named in honor of the great master.[368] In the scientific and medical fields mention should be made of the library of Wilhelm Baum (died 1883) of Göttingen, probably the finest private surgical collection of Germany with its numerous works from the fifteenth, sixteenth, and seventeenth centuries, of the equally important library of Emil Du Bois-Reymond (died 1896), both of which went to the Newberry Library, and finally the library of the bacteriologist Karl Flugge containing more than 13,000 reprints which went to the University of Chicago.[369]

But many German or German-American scholars also built up on American soil considerable libraries which they usually willed or presented to their universities. One might recall Hugo Münsterberg whose gigantic library of more than 10,000 volumes was presented to Harvard College in 1917.[370] Similarly, Professor A. C. Coolidge, director of the Harvard Library, commemorated the visit of Prince Heinrich of Prussia by establishing the Hohenzollern Library of Harvard and equipping it with more than 11,000 volumes.[371] By gift, legacy, and purchase the great German scientific periodicals, serials, and polygraphic works in particular were acquired by American libraries. They are even to be found in the smaller and medium-sized college libraries, often in an astonishing quantity.

It was inevitable that the migration of complete sets of manuscripts and incunabula should stimulate the prices considerably and thereby prevent German libraries from competing any longer with American purchasers. Towards the turn of the century there was obvious concern in the German library world as well as among the general public. Articles on the emigration of German libraries appeared in the daily press.[372] At the German library meeting of 1904 Schwenke spoke about the matter, and in 1907 Milkau spoke forthrightly of an American peril. However, a man as well informed on German and American research librarianship as Richard Pietschmann pointed out that the great research libraries would hardly be damaged since the emigrating scholars' libraries held little not already in the former and that in no case could the state library administration be reproached.[373] But when the selling went on and on after World War I and irreplaceable items and collections (among others large portions of the princely family library of the Stolberg-Wernigerodes) had to be sold in America to satisfy immediate necessity, state intervention to protect German collections finally became necessary. Nevertheless it must be admitted that by far the larger part of these older and more recent German family and scholars' libraries have found worthy homes in American libraries.[374] Many have been kept together as special collections under the names of their founders, and all have left clearly perceptible traces on the collections into which they have been incorporated.

COLLEGE AND UNIVERSITY LIBRARIES

By comparison with the great European university libraries the American counterparts were very modest about 1876 and remained so until the end of the century.[375] Only Harvard had a collection of more than 200,000 volumes. Yale had almost reached the 100,000 mark, a few libraries had between 20,000 and 40,000, while the great majority could call only a few thousand volumes their own.[376] As late as the next decade libraries of more than 50,000 volumes were available for use by only 8 per cent of all students, while 43 per cent had to be satisfied with libraries of less than 5,000 volumes. Incomes were also quite insufficient. Only the older libraries had their own investments amounting to $25,000 or more, and Harvard alone had been able to collect a library endowment of almost $170,000. But most libraries were dependent upon occasional endowments and in general had to turn to subscriptions and fees. Book funds hovered between a few hundred and several thousand dollars. In reality only the libraries of the endowed universities had regular fixed incomes, while the state universities and colleges depended upon less pretentious governmental appropriations, which in turn were reapportioned annually by the president according to total needs.

Building conditions were unsatisfactory, in many cases even pitiful. Frequently the reading room was separated from the library and at times left to student supervision.[377] Most libraries were not very accessible, for hours were limited to a brief daily period or definite days of the week. Correspondingly the circulation statistics were rather low.[378] In the administration the influence of the faculty was predominant. Either the president or a committee appointed by him exercised supervision, and as late as 1890 almost two-thirds of all libraries were directed by professors as a side line or by committees.

A peculiar, quite fundamental difference between American academic libraries and related European institutions has always existed in the fact that their holdings represent in no way the whole of the arts and sciences. In accordance with the purpose of the college within the American university of introducing the student only to general studies, leaving intensive study after the baccalaureate to professional and graduate schools of the university, the college library has set as its goal from the very beginning the collection of general literature, while special and scholarly works are left to departmental and collegiate libraries. Of the 32,000 volumes of Columbia University in 1875 only 19,000 belonged to the college library.[379] The University of Michigan Library was composed entirely of departmental libraries with 23,000 volumes in all. In Chicago, according to the plan of President Harper, the research institutes and laboratories were to be operated in conjunction with libraries;[380] and there was actually no university library until 1912, for it existed only as the sum total of books in the departmental libraries.[381] Separately shelved collections were most numerous at Harvard. In 1880 there were eighteen departmental and seven house libraries with full independence; and they were not placed under the jurisdiction of the director of the libraries until 1912, while other more recent specialized libraries remained independent. In time most separately shelved collections such as those at Yale, Princeton, Cornell, California, and elsewhere, were united with the main library, without, however, being completely swallowed up.

By the last decade of the nineteenth century a rather complicated system of libraries had been formed at most colleges and universities. It consisted of collections of the most varied types, origins, and purposes and a highly questionable administrative organization resulting in division of funds and responsibility for acquisition. Thanks to the handsome new buildings constructed after 1900 the development of specialized libraries was forced into closer coordination with the university library, and a central library appeared on the campus of the university.

Monumental buildings, the first of which was California's in 1912, were erected in the following decades and proclaimed the position of the library as the intellectual heart of the university. But neither well-rounded collections nor the necessary level of holdings were attained by this measure. The approximately forty university libraries of the present day are still plagued by the weaknesses resulting from their origins in the collections of liberal arts colleges and from gradually absorbing collections of the various disciplines as opportunity presented itself. Unlike the German universities, they were not permitted to carry out a planned expansion of holdings in all fields. W. W. Bishop was forced to complain that around 1900 there were hardly three or four university libraries which were in a position to provide the necessary literary sources for serious research.[382] To be sure, much has happened since that date; but even within the last decade a statistical investigation was published on the holdings of college libraries, revealing that only a few contained research material and that the great majority held only books for instructional purposes.[383]

Special Libraries and Research Libraries

Much more distinctive were the special and research libraries which sprang up everywhere in the nineteenth century, either outside of the universities or in loose conjunction with them. With the beginning of the twentieth century they developed into a special category by virtue of the extent and significance of their holdings. Corporate, private, official, and municipal groups all participated in their growth. The older special libraries of the legal corporations and law schools, the institutions offering theological instruction and the seminaries, the medical schools and hospitals have already been mentioned. In addition a number of special scientific libraries, for example those of the Academy of Natural Sciences in Philadelphia (1812), the Cambridge Museum of Comparative Zoology

(1858),[384] the Smithsonian Institution, and the Peabody Museum in Baltimore (1857) have existed for purposes of research from the very beginning. In Jewett's annual reports for the Smithsonian Institution the absence of bibliographic tools, specialized literature, and standard European works is lamented time and again; and Thomas Gill, a co-worker on the report of 1876, complained that the masterpieces of zoological literature were not in Washington and that he had not even been able to lay his hands on a copy of *Justs Botanischer Jahresbericht*.[385] As late as 1900 the Library of Congress owned scarcely more than 20,000 volumes in the biological sciences and perhaps 15,000 volumes in mathematics, physics, and chemistry. However, the scientific research worker had at his disposal such departmental libraries as those of the U.S. Department of Agriculture or the Bureau of Mines which, as a result of these demands, had developed research libraries in their own fields. A few years later the endowed John Crerar Library was opened (1897), and today, with about 700,000 volumes, it occupies the first place among the scientific libraries of the country.

But most significant was the rise of special technical libraries, which had had their forerunners in the early nineteenth century, but became prominent only in its last decades. In 1881 Carnegie erected his first public library in Pittsburgh, and the first technological division, opened there in 1889, has developed into one of the most successful in the country. In the same year S. S. Green had discussed the theme of libraries and technology for the first time at the American Library Association conference.[386] Soon the other great industrial cities followed suit with the establishment of technological institutes and libraries. Thanks to the labors of John Cotton Dana[387] and the example of his library in Newark more and more public libraries adopted the plan of opening special divisions and branches for technology. This phenomenon was not limited to technology but affected other fields as well. The New York Public Library was gradually split up into twenty departments held together only by the Reference Department. In Cleveland (1913) and finally in Baltimore (1932) the development was carried even further with the establishment of special reading rooms with corresponding stack sections for the various departments. The Special Libraries Association was founded in 1902 upon Dana's inspiration, and starting with forty member libraries, it includes more than 3,000 today.[388]

If the beginning of the public library was the first step towards democratization of libraries, then the special library signified the beginning of the mobilization and rationalization of specialized literature. This circumstance required new and more refined methods of acquisition and care. With the new groups of patrons there also appeared a new type of library administrator, the special librarian, and not alone in the special libraries of the municipalities and universities, to administer the special collections and special divisions. The establishment of five "library chairs" and fourteen "library consultantships" in the Library of Congress for definitely specialized fields and for expert advice to patrons also shows America's national library on its way toward the destiny of a modern research library.[389]

The generosity of private collectors has clearly been the leitmotiv in the history of American librarianship;[390] and, what is even more important, the growth of the best research libraries in the nation is due to their industry and zeal as collectors. Quite apart from famous collections which passed into the hands of public or academic libraries—such as the Astor and Lenox library, the John Carter Brown collection of Americana in Providence (1900), the E. E. Ayer collection of American Indian material in the Newberry Library in Chicago (1911), the Hoover War Library at Stanford, the Harry Elkins Widener collection at Harvard (1913), to mention but a few—a long list of private collections have passed into public ownership in recent years, many of them unique not merely because of their incredible wealth but also because of their purpose. Above all there is the Henry E. Huntington Library in San Marino, one of the richest of all collections of incunabula and English and American imprints. In 1925 it was opened as a research institution, and it employs with endowment funds special research workers whose investigations are reported in its own journal (since 1931), in facsimiles, and other publications. In addition there is the William L. Clements Library in Ann Arbor (1923) with its rich collections in early American history, the W. A. Clark Memorial Library in Los Angeles (1926), excellent for English literature, the Pierpont Morgan Library in New York, famous for its costly manuscripts and incunabula and dedicated in 1924 to the promotion of knowledge and the patronage of scholars from all parts of the world. One of the youngest and most select is the Folger Shakespeare Library in Washington which Henry Clay Folger gave to the American people in 1932 as a Shakespeare memorial and as a unique institute for Shakespearean research.[391]

THE PUBLIC LIBRARIES

No period of history has been so favorable to urban and rural libraries of the United States as the last quarter of the nineteenth and the first quarter of the twentieth century. The 3,682 public libraries reported in 1876 were increased to 5,300 by 1900. Total holdings had mounted from 12,000,000 to 44,000,000 volumes, of which New York alone had 7,500,00, Massachusetts 6,000,000, and Pennsylvania 4,000,000.[392] Various forces coincided to attain this end. The population and importance of American cities increased rapidly. In 1860 16 per cent of the population lived in cities with more than 8,000 inhabitants, and by 1900 this proportion had mounted to 32 per cent. Of the thirty-nine cities with more than 100,000 inhabitants, fifteen had more than 250,000 and three had passed the million mark. The school systems went forward rapidly, for the number of secondary schools alone increased from 100 in 1860 to 2,500 in 1890 and 7,000 by 1900. In 1890 they were attended by 200,000 pupils; in 1900 by 500,000. When the ten-hour day was legally established after 1850 and the eight-hour day after 1890, the people were able to spend leisure time in educational institutions and libraries.[393]

By 1880 all states had passed library laws, and after 1890 most states had adopted a plan for preparing the way for rural library facilities by their own library commissions. The American Library Association, under such distinguished presidents as Winsor, Cutter, Poole, and Dana, to mention only a few, and under the forceful influence of Melvil Dewey, and the library movement in general gained in scope and strength. Yet in 1875 half of all public libraries had to be supported by subscription, endowment, and other such sources; and even in 1900 appropriations from taxes were far less than what was needed. Even in Boston the library tax yielded only fifty cents per person, in Chicago fifteen cents, and in New York barely nine cents, while municipal appropriations for schools amounted on the average to four dollars per person.[394]

Perhaps the beginning of the golden age of public libraries would have been delayed even longer had not one man, Andrew Carnegie,[395] in grateful memory of youthful impressions of a lending library, decided to spend his tremendous fortune on the erection of library buildings. Carnegie was convinced that of all benevolences the library is the greatest, since it gives nothing without demanding something in return and helps only those who are willing to help themselves. Accordingly he set forth one absolute prerequisite for his gift: an annual contribution from the community for the support of the library of at least 10 per cent of the cost of the building. The erection of 1,677 Carnegie buildings in 1,408 localities during the period 1896-1923 is surely a unique event in history of libraries; and the most impressive document of this period is probably the letter of March 12, 1901 which Carnegie wrote to John Shaw Billings, director of the New York Public Library, announcing the gift of $5,200,000 for the erection of sixty-five branch libraries. He wrote, "Sixty-five libraries at one stroke probably breaks the record, but this is the day of great operations and New York is soon to be the biggest of cities."[396] In January 1911 Carnegie handed over the further administration of his philanthropic enterprises to a corporation bearing his name. Gradually the Carnegie Corporation of New York extended its activities to all branches of librarianship, to promotion of the American Library Association's program, to publication of bibliographies and works dealing with library science, to education for librarianship and improvement of library schools. Since there was no headquarters for libraries up until the recent past, the Carnegie Corporation, without any official appointment, performed the actual functions of an advisory group, whose cooperation in all matters of library policy was all the more valuable because action usually followed close on the heels of advice.[397]

Carnegie's activity fell in the period when the great American fortunes were established. And together with him as well as after him American millionaires have felt obligated to the nation to leave schools, museums, art galleries, and libraries to the nation which gave them their wealth, even though it might be only to perpetuate their fame in future generations. And in point of fact the names of Astor, Lenox, Tilden, John Carter Brown, Fiske, Crerar, Newberry, Rockefeller, Morgan, Folger, Huntington, Sterling, Widener, and Mellon signify a corresponding number of imposing libraries[398] with incredible treasures, and, what is even more important, just as many centers of active research. Innumerable other philanthropists might be named, and there are probably few cities and communities in the United States who have not had occasion to commemorate large or small endowments in connection with the history of their libraries. Whatever the motives, whatever the effects—not always desirable— of the library endowments, they have left their stamp on American librarianship since 1890 and have given the American librarian opportunity to develop techniques and routine work to a point of perfection. In a word, they have made America a wonderland of libraries.

LIBRARY SYSTEMS AND LIBRARY EXTENSION

The perfection and modernization of the American public library falls in the decades after 1890. Externally the development was characterized by such fine new buildings as those at Boston (1890), New York (1911), Cleveland (1913), Los Angeles (1926), Philadelphia (1927), and Baltimore (1932), each of which represents at once the formation of a distinct type of library. The development of the organization may be illustrated in catchwords: consolidation of the municipal systems; formation of branch, travelling, and county libraries; library extension and adult education. The details of the development were naturally influenced by earlier initiative and local circumstances. Wherever there was already an older library (as in Boston) which combined a scientific reference section with a popular lending division, it was not too difficult to adapt the field of activity to growing demands. It was a happy coincidence that in 1905 the directorship of the first great municipal library fell into the hands of Herbert Putnam who succeeded in building a library system with fifteen branches and fifty-six delivery stations within four years.[399]

Likewise, wherever there were no older competitive collections, such as in St. Louis, Cincinnati, or other western cities, it was easier to develop a municipal system of central, branch, and school libraries than in cities where there were already older and vital social, society, and special libraries. In many cities there was a consolidation of smaller libraries into a central library after the nineties.

However, in such older library centers as Philadelphia, Baltimore, New York, and elsewhere, either the non-municipal libraries continued to exist (as in Boston) or the public library movement was unable to force its right of way until relatively late. Perhaps New York[400] was in the most difficult position of all, for there the great collections of Astor and Lenox attracted all serious scholarly investigation almost until the end of the century. They represented an important factor in the intellectual life of the city but discouraged new ideas by their old-fashioned predilections. Similarly there was scarcely one of the numerous society and special libraries which could have been the basis for a great municipal library with the possible exception of the Free Circulating Library (founded in 1879) which, with its eleven branches, attended to the library needs of the metropolis until 1900. Accordingly it was an event of more than local significance when the Astor, Lenox, and Tilden foundations were combined with the Circulating Library in 1901 and the new public library building was opened in 1911. What is today the greatest public library in the world has also carried the idea of a unified metropolitan library to its greatest perfection.

Following the style set by Boston, where the first branch library had been established in 1870, the public libraries of the rapidly growing cities surrounded themselves with a network of branches and delivery stations in the ensuing decades.[401] Under the influence of the Carnegie foundations the branch library became an established institution even in towns and villages, while in the great cities reckoning their population in millions there were many branches and often more than a hundred deposit collections in clubs, business firms, factories, fire and police stations, hospitals, barracks, ships, and even in jails. In addition, the schools once more proved themselves to be very adaptable media for library extension, when state laws provided for the establishment of deposit collections and travelling libraries after 1889.[402] After 1897 the special Library Extension Division was established by the New York State Education Department, and from this kernel the greatest travelling library system in the world was formed, providing for schools and for juvenile and adult readers of all classes of the population.

The remarkable thing about the municipal library systems is the flexibility and originality with which they were able in most cases to assure the acquisition, preparation, and distribution of reading material for the far-flung districts of American cities with their multiplicity of geographical, industrial, and demographic elements and the frequent alteration of their social structure. That such an organization also represents a significant administrative accomplishment is obvious when one realizes that the American city is a highly complicated administrative entity and that the municipal central library itself is not one unit but rather a combination of numerous elements of various types. Furthermore, it is dependent upon the cooperation of quite unrelated bureaus, committees, and corporations, upon the circumstances of shifting economic and financial conditions, and upon the observance of countless municipal and state laws and regulations.[403] The mastery of such organizational problems, for which there is hardly a parallel in Europe with the possible exception of England, must be viewed as one of the great accomplishments of the American public library.

County library service met with similar administrative difficulties from the beginning.[404] While the smaller towns with not less than 10,000 inhabitants were usually in a position to support their own public libraries, the villages and the counties were forced to depend upon school-district libraries, travelling libraries, or the library systems of nearby cities. After 1898 came legislation in the individual states, first of all in Ohio, which permitted the levying of taxes for library purposes. Of more than 3,000 counties in the country, only about 230 have taken advantage of this opportunity to date. In the Midwest and Far West the movement has been stronger than in the East and the South. The most successful state has been California, where a model system of county libraries was established after 1909. It even included large cities like Fresno and parts of Los Angeles. Without going into the highly complicated relationships and administrative position of the districts and their libraries and into the lines of demarcation between their authority and that of other types of libraries, it is only possible here to emphasize one significant aspect of recent trends. Often county and municipal libraries are so close that, in view of the community to be served, a far reaching cooperation, "regionalism," has come into existence. It extends beyond local and state authority and seems to be destined to play an important role in provision of library service for the great "neglected regions," in the execution of cooperative enterprises and of a general library policy.[405]

According to W. W. Bishop the public library primarily serves the purpose of securing books for the recreation and information of the average reader.[406] If the public library feels that it is an immediate educational agency, the origin of this idea is rooted in the first half of the nineteenth century, indeed, actually as early as Franklin's day. The belief in the educational and cultural power of the book inspired generations of colonists and pioneers on the great movement westward, and the original lack of schools and bookstores made the library the confederate of all cultural goals in both large and small cities.[407] The rise of the schools signalled the appearance of school libraries, and the public libraries looked upon library provision for youth and for adult workers as the natural continuation of formal education.

In the beginning of the nineties Melvil Dewey came out for participation of libraries in the university extension movement with the enthusiasm of a seer. This movement began with the founding of the University of Chicago in 1892 and aimed at the spread of higher education through evening and outside schools, correspondence courses, and special training.[408] But an independent library extension movement came into existence only after World War I[409] and under the influence of the social changes in its backwash. Under the leadership of the American Library Association the public, university, and college libraries took part in the movement, which, under the name of adult education, was actively supported by universities, teachers' organizations, women's clubs, and other national groups. Libraries were not satisfied with helping by compiling reading lists, giving information, arranging special rooms for meetings, and many other nominal services, but they also took an active part in the cultural life of the cities by giving advisory service for readers, preparing programs, evening reading and discussion groups, professional courses, lectures, radio courses, and play production. The public library discovered its mission in the social and cultural life of the nation; for the password "adult education" plays a role in the program of the large and even medium-sized libraries and has actually found a place in the curriculum of the library schools.

But there has been no dearth of criticism even in library circles concerning the value of these enterprises. It is argued that the public takes no part in them and that they are ignored by sociologists. Likewise it is claimed that the public library has been unable to increase the number of readers by any considerable figure since the seventies, and 70 per cent of the readers still prefer lighter books. Nowhere save in Boston and a few other cities has there been a "book-minded leisure class" of any importance.[410] On the other hand, the recognized accomplishments of the public library in the recent depression years[411] must be emphasized as much as the "Americanization" of foreigners and library provision for youth and children. But perhaps the public library has accomplished one of its finest and most permanent tasks after decades of effort in the libraries of the villages and towns where it has contributed to the intellectual and cultural enrichment of life in these lonely and monotonous communities.

CHAPTER NINE

INNER STRUCTURE

GROWTH OF COLLECTIONS[412]

One can scarcely speak of systematically growing collections in the colonial period because acquisition followed no definite principles but increased only as it was possible through gift, endowment, and other means. In the college libraries selection of books was prescribed by the curriculum, but most acquisitions were made from income from taxes, fees, fines, and the sale of duplicates. Everywhere the results were modest. If the nature of books collected in the different types of libraries during the seventeenth and eighteenth centuries were broadly characterized, it would be found that theological, classical, legal, and philosophical literature was prominent in college libraries, scientific literature in society and subscription libraries, belles-lettres and rare and valuable works largely in private libraries. Society and academic libraries of the nineteenth century collected mostly didactic works and serious and lighter pleasure reading, a policy which was adopted and continued by the public libraries. A systematic plan of acquisition was more widely followed during the second half of the nineteenth century by the municipal libraries. The reference section demanded more consideration for practical books, reference works, and manuals. In addition, many special collections arose, for example, in the field of local and regional history. In the large libraries these collections are hardly to be distinguished from the ones which are found in the reading rooms of university libraries. Towards the end of the century and particularly after 1900 there was a rising specialization which also had its effect here, for the larger municipal libraries established their special divisions, whose nature and scope were determined by local conditions and fortuitous circumstances. Technology, industry, and commerce were cultivated everywhere where there was money, but art, music, drama, and many other fields were also given special attention.

The establishment of the general and lending collections reflects the times, the people, and the conditions.[413] There were not only the great events of American history, the Revolution, the frontier and pioneer age, emancipation, the War Between the States, industrialism, and international politics, which always represented a large proportion of acquisitions, but also social, religious, and racial problems. Waves of European and Asiatic immigration bore the literary heritage of the old world to the libraries of the east and west coasts and deep into the continent. But the dominant factor in this growth was the novel and light literature; and almost from the beginning of the public libraries they assumed leading positions maintained up to the present day as revealed in statistics of acquisition and lending. The arguments to justify the position of fiction concerned libraries, patrons, and supervisory officers less than the question of whether the theory of value or of use should have the upper hand in the policy of acquisition. As long as 70 to 80 per cent of the clientele of American libraries belongs to the category of fiction readers,[414] acquisition will lean one-sidedly in this direction both at present and in the future.

American libraries, unlike their European sisters, were unable to take over the old and valuable holdings of dissolved or suppressed collections. But many of the rare and unique items of old world literature that went on the market have been acquired by American collectors and agents for the new world. Even in recent times Morgan, Huntington, Henry Walters, and others have been able to acquire collections of manuscripts and incunabula which, together with a long list of ornamental pieces, represent nearly all types of medieval schools and early printing houses.[415] Since Henry Stevens began his quests for Americana, numerous American libraries have labored to assure the preservation of early documents of political and cultural life; and with the help of photography this material can be supplemented by whatever is preserved in English archives and libraries.

The Library of Congress, which appeared on the scene too late to compete with the British Museum or even with the private collectors, has at least been able to secure an almost complete collection of historical literature published since about 1870, and after 1900 it was also able to acquire older Americana. After 1846 the Library of Congress received two copies of all works published in the United States with the exception of temporary interruptions and restrictions, and since 1870 it has enjoyed full copyright privileges.[416] The system of international exchange which has existed since 1867 has brought the Library of Congress official documents of most countries and numerous society publications, but not the valuable works published under official subsidies. The real growth of the national library began only with the opening of the new building and the appointment of Herbert Putnam as librarian on April 5, 1899. During the next forty years the library's holdings were expanded from 1,000,000 to about 6,000,000 volumes, not counting manuscripts, maps, plans, pictures, and engravings.[417] The unique accomplishment of the Library of Congress lies in the fact that, despite relatively modest funds and without noteworthy endowments before 1925, it has been in the position to offer the "unusual book for the unusual problem" in most fields and to serve the entire nation as a research library which rarely fails to satisfy a request.

The universities have not been so fortunate in building up their holdings. In many fields their lacunae were lamentable up to 1900; and as late as 1912 it was revealed by a standard list of source materials for European history that Harvard was in a satisfactory position but that not even half the titles existed in any other library. The weakness of college libraries has already been pointed out.[418] The strength of the academic libraries, even in the smaller colleges, lies in the frequently astonishing number of valuable special collections and in the long runs of periodicals and society publications. But most college and university libraries have lacked both money and labor necessary for the planned construction of a unified and universal collection. Justin Winsor had already pointed out in 1876 the dangers of aimless collecting and the resultant competition.[419] Likewise the rich flow of funds since 1900 was often used without conscious purpose and under the most haphazard circumstances. "Apparently," wrote W. W. Bishop as late as 1938, "all the big libraries of the United States have gone on the supposition that each one of them would develop into a British Museum or a Library of Congress."[420]

Proposals for cooperation and division of fields of emphasis were made repeatedly, but to date there have been only vestigial beginnings of such agreements, for example, the one between Minnesota, Michigan, and Illinois concerning the purchase of publications from European academies and societies.[421]

On the other hand, in building up the special libraries, private as well as business and governmental, there has usually been the greatest consistency, and particularly in recent years there has been an effort to build up adequate research libraries. Technological and commercial libraries occupy a special place in this field because they frequently point toward and attain completeness. A good example is the Engineering Societies Library in New York which originated in 1913-16 through the consolidation of the four largest engineering societies' libraries and owns what is probably the greatest collection of technological periodicals in the world.[422]

But the greatest inequalities existed in the distribution of libraries over the various sections of the country. Libraries were most numerous along the Atlantic seaboard, the Great Lakes, and the Far West, while the South and the Southwest were the great neglected regions. This condition reflects the general course of America's cultural development. Further differentiation appeared at the beginning of the twentieth century. Special libraries were concentrated in the industrial regions of the eastern, midwestern, and far western states, scientific research libraries principally in the Northeast, and the great collections of federal bureaus in Washington. On the whole there was a remarkably impressive augmentation of holdings after 1876. The number of libraries increased from 3,682 to about 10,000, but total holdings mounted from about 12,000,000 to 200,000,000![423]

CATALOGUES[424]

The colonial period produced no cataloguing technique simply because there were no libraries sufficiently large to cause cataloguing problems. One might expect little concern for cataloguing problems in America, for in eighteenth-century Germany in the same period, with the sole exception of Göttingen, no definite practice, even for the alphabetical catalogue, had been formulated. Those catalogues of colonial libraries which were drawn up and printed followed English models, that is, with a classified arrangement according to the disciplines and within these divisions alphabetically according to authors or even according to the shelving locations, often with an appended author index.

To be sure, the first half of the nineteenth century brought a more intensive concern for order and listing in libraries, but there were still no cataloguing rules. In the Library of Congress the first catalogue was prepared in 1802, and by 1876 it had been succeeded by sixty partial or complete catalogues.[425] The policy of most libraries was to print their catalogues; and when the Bureau of Education report of 1876 lists 1,010 printed catalogues (382 later than 1870), this circumstance reveals less a highly perfected cataloguing practice than a general misunderstanding of cataloguing problems. Printing means the end, not the continuation of development. Harvard alone had discarded this practice as early as 1834 and adopted the manuscript sheaf catalogue which was divided into author and subject catalogues in 1861.[426]

A significant step forward in cataloguing was the proposal of Charles C. Jewett, who laid his plans before the Smithsonian Institution in 1851 and later before the general public. It involved the preparation of a central catalogue by using stereotyped plates, a pioneer attempt to solve this problem. It failed because of technical imperfections and Jewett's retirement from office.[427] However, Jewett had already realized that uniform rules were a prerequisite for centralized cataloguing; and, under the influence of Panizzi's ninety-one rules he drew up the first American code, which has also become the basis for the later rules. Likewise, it was Jewett who recommended a combination of the two customary types of catalogues (author and subject) and thereby laid the basis for the American dictionary catalogue.

Neither was uniformity in cataloguing attained by isolated cases of exemplary work;[428] but the way was pointed out when Charles A. Cutter published his *Rules for a Printed Dictionary Catalogue,* based on Jewett's proposals, as the second part of the report of 1876.[429] Likewise, the American Library Association—and Melvil Dewey in particular—labored to assure uniform entries and Anglo-American cooperation. As early as 1877 the initial feelers were sent out to British librarians, and in 1878 Dewey issued a committee proposal for rules. In 1890 the first American code was published, and in 1900 the American Library Association established a special cataloguers' division for further revision of the rules. When J. C. M. Hanson, head of the Library of Congress catalogue department after 1897, took over the direction of this work, the common code of *Anglo-American Rules* was finished in 1907 after long conferences with English librarians and published the following year.[430]

The Anglo-American code aimed at the creation of uniform entries for a card catalogue, called international, although restricted to the two countries, and designed to serve all libraries. The Library Bureau in Boston, founded by Melvil Dewey, had been publishing printed catalogue cards since 1886, and after 1898 the American Library Association carried on the work. But a decisive turn of events occurred at this time, for the Library of Congress began printing its cards. Before the nineties the national library could hardly have boasted of its catalogues. The first subject catalogue had appeared between 1864 and 1869, and the first author catalogue was begun in 1878 but remained a torso. Later, cataloguing on cards was adopted, but for the lack of an established tradition it was not possible to bring any order to the catalogue of the rapidly growing library.[431] A new catalogue begun in 1898 using cards of international format was based on modified rules and arranged in dictionary form. The old author catalogue had been stopped in 1900, and Herbert Putnam went back to Jewett's plan for central cataloguing and began printing cards in 1901. Exchange agreements were reached with libraries which already printed cards, and in 1902 distribution to so-called depository libraries was begun. The American Library Association stopped printing cards, and the Library of Congress now took over all the tasks of central cataloguing and of a bibliographical center for the entire land. The number of subscribers, originally small, gradually increased through the propagandistic efforts of the chief of the card division, Charles H. Hastings.[432] The smaller and even the large libraries recognized the advantages of cooperation with the Library of Congress for the administration, improvement, and simplification of their own cataloguing. The central cataloguing was carefully based on a long file of handbooks, instructions, and rules. At present there are some 6,000 subscribers, and fifty-eight American and fourteen foreign libraries receive all cards as depository libraries.

One result of the cooperation of the Library of Congress with card-printing libraries was a union catalogue,[433] which was placed on a sound basis by a Rockefeller grant and has become the most formidable bibliographical tool in the nation with its no less than 10,000,000 titles built up by gradual inclusion of eighty-four libraries' holdings which are not duplicated in the Library of Congress. Since 1935 the Union Catalogue has also served as the basis for a national information bureau for locations and the beginnings of a system of interlibrary loan. Also since 1935 other union catalogues for limited regions have arisen; and although their immediate objectives were local, they have nevertheless moved in the same direction, toward the inclusion of all books in the country and toward national cooperation.[434]

The cataloguing work of the Library of Congress has had a fundamental formative influence on American librarianship. Also of decisive importance, at least for the Library of Congress and most research libraries, was the new classification[435] worked out after 1897 by Charles Martel and Stefan Stefansson. In 1909 it replaced the old classification which harked back to Jefferson's day and included only forty-four divisions. To date it has been adopted by 200 American libraries and a few in Europe. It is a continuation of Cutter's expansive classification (1891), and like Dewey's system (1876), is a shelving system rather than the basis for classified catalogues, which in America are almost nonexistent. Dewey's system is used in about 89 per cent of American libraries, replacing the older method of shelving by large, subdivided subject groups with fixed places; but neither it, the Library of Congress system, the Cutter system, nor any other classification have been able to displace the chief types of American catalogues, the subject and the dictionary.

BUILDINGS, ARCHITECTURE AND INTERIOR DESIGN[436]

There were no difficulties involved in housing libraries in the seventeenth and eighteenth centuries, and consequently there were no investigations of the problem. At the end of the colonial period the largest college library of the period was shelved in typically English style in ten decorative alcoves of beautiful Harvard Hall. Gore Hall, Harvard's first library building, was constructed between 1838 and 1841 on the model of King's Chapel in Cambridge; but after thirty years it was so full that a book wing, the first stack in America, was added. This was the beginning of a series of expansions,[437] which ended only with the construction of the Widener Library in 1912-15. Harvard's experiences were repeated in all the great libraries because the extent and the tempo of growth were underestimated. When the Boston Public Library was expanded in 1860, it was thought that a building designed to contain 200,000 volumes would be satisfactory for a hundred years. These figures were already superannuated by 1876; and accordingly the building of 1890, the first modern library building, was planned for tenfold expansion. When Congress decided in 1873 to draw up plans for a new building for the Library of Congress, the librarian, A. R. Spofford, had estimated in 1875 that the existing collection of 250,000 volumes would be doubled in twenty years. The library passed the half-million mark in eight years and had reached its first million by the time it was moved into the new building.[438] When the era of great libraries began in the nineties, the lesson of these experiences had been learned, and it was now attempted to meet future space shortages by more and more monumental buildings.

Justin Winsor was the first to investigate architectural questions, even though he was primarily concerned with interior arrangements. In his contribution to the report of 1876 he introduced a plan for a library of 1,000,000 volumes with seven tiers and a logical arrangement of public and staff rooms.[439] Winsor had already come to the conclusion, completely at variance with opinions of architects and library committees, that a library building for a city must be designed differently from one for such an institution as an antiquarian society; and he complained that there were already too many architectural monstrosities. The decade between 1890 and 1900 was a turning point in these matters.[440] Public libraries were influenced by the Carnegie endowments which favored a standard type with far reaching uniformity in plans and equipment.

New buildings of municipal, college, and university libraries, which were erected before and after 1900 together with other public buildings as a kind of gesture of the maturity of American imperialism, were executed under the influence of the neoclassicism summoned forth by the Chicago Fair of 1893. The college and university libraries, which had cultivated the Tudor style throughout the nineteenth century (in the South the colonial style), were dominated from now on by a type of structure accentuated by the massive columns supporting the portico, the gigantic steps at the entrance, and the lofty space-consuming corridors. The great municipal libraries inclined more to the heavy Renaissance style, to the finished building often topped by a glazed dome. But many libraries expressed a more or less regional peculiarity, a tendency especially noticeable in the Spanish character of the large libraries of the West and Southwest and of the bungalow type of small ones in the same region. The large buildings of recent decades were inspired by a practical architectural tendency, and Yale alone has copied historic English elements in its own capricious interpretation. Skyscrapers and book towers, such as those of Pittsburgh and Texas, represent the appearance of a totally new architectural element.

But America's contribution to the development of library architecture has been even more typical and epoch-making in the interior design of the building than in exterior styles. This development came to fruition in the last four decades, perhaps even more rapidly in the public libraries than in the university libraries. It involved two problems, the position of the stack relative to the building as a whole and the functional differentiation of public rooms. Poole had already begun the establishment of departments in the Newberry Library in 1887 and later in the Boston Public Library. In the first carefully planned, modern university library, the Wisconsin State Historical Library (1895), there was provision for seminar and study rooms. The Providence Public Library (1900) was the first to carry out the complete separation of the reference department from other divisions. Very extensive departmentalization was employed in the New York Public Library (1911), and the Cleveland Public Library (1913) went to even greater extremes. Both present a complex of mutually supplementary departments with separate reading rooms, all serving the multiplicity of functions of the great municipal library. In the great buildings of the postwar period, for example, Los Angeles (1926), Philadelphia (1927), and Baltimore (1932), the conception of departmentalization attained its final form. The Enoch Pratt Free Library in Baltimore is split up into separate collections and reading rooms, but with the greatest clarity, ease of supervision, and efficiency.

The tendency towards centralization was stronger in the university libraries, and it was expressed particularly in the retention of the monumental central reading room, although its powers of attraction were no longer as strong as those of buildings with special reading rooms, seminar rooms, and particularly the almost constantly overcrowded reserve book rooms. Still the tendency towards decentralization which was innate in university library policy as a whole was recognized in the library of Johns Hopkins (1876), later in Chicago's Harper Memorial Library (1911), and above all in Yale's Sterling Library (1925). The tendency toward specialization enjoyed genuine triumphs in all modern university libraries in the study and seminar rooms and carrels. In such libraries as California (1912), Widener (1915), Minnesota (1924), and Columbia's South Hall (1934, renamed Nicholas Murray Butler Hall in 1946), the building was a core surrounded by hundreds of appendages, apparently a denial of unity and supervision, but technically well administered and closely controlled.

The university libraries have also been less extravagant than the municipal libraries in consuming space with excessively large staircases, a fault not even avoided by Widener. In place of the stairs they have put the great loan desk (e.g., University of Southern California, 1932), and in general they have aimed at concentration represented by economical use of space and shortening of lines of communication (e.g., Michigan, Minnesota, and Columbia). Munthe has praised Dartmouth's Baker Memorial Library (1928) for attaining at once the height of utility and beauty.[441]

The position and function of the stack is perhaps one of the most difficult problems of library architecture, and American libraries have provided a wealth of interesting and instructive examples. Aside from a few magnificent examples of hall libraries with galleries (e.g., Boston Athenaeum, and Peabody Institute, Baltimore),

American libraries constructed since 1890 are exclusively the stack type, usually a rectangular building incorporating a stack block (less frequently a stack wing). The stack has made a kind of an odyssey from the periphery to the center of the building, and in many instances it has been virtually dissolved at this point. The progressive moves which brought the mass of books closer and closer to the points of use were made possible by advances in illumination, ventilation, temperature control, and the desired independence from all external physical conditions. This route can perhaps be traced functionally, although not chronologically, in the following examples: stack at the rear of the building (New York Public), at the rear and on the sides (Widener), center of the lower tiers (Butler Hall), as a block in the center (Sterling), partially dispersed (Pratt), or completely dispersed (Cleveland). The only further development, of a somewhat different nature, may be seen in the towers at Texas, Pittsburgh, and Dartmouth where the administrative quarters and reading rooms surround the stack as a shell or are drawn inward by floors. This tendency was followed most consistently in the Library of Congress Annex (1938) where the twelve-tier stack is surrounded on all sides by offices and study rooms and the great catalogue and reading rooms are on the uppermost tier.[442]

THE LIBRARY PROFESSION[443]

James Logan demanded in his will of 1750 that the librarian be competent in translation and analysis of Latin classics, comprehension of the New Testament, Homer, and Hesiod in the original Greek. In later years standards have been considerably lowered, for in 1876 an academic education and competence in Latin and Greek were considered sufficient, and the ability to read Herodotus and Horace at sight was not required.[444] And at that time, as well as twenty-five years later, there were many unsuccessful clergymen, lawyers without a practice, incompetent teachers, physicians without patients, and other failures who wanted to become librarians.[445] Even today librarianship is open to anyone who can show a minimum of formal education acquired from the high school and a few years of college. However, any attempt to generalize on the basis of such phenomena would give an altogether false picture of the situation. The character of the librarian has shifted with the changing times. Today, professional morale and education are perhaps no less profound and at all events more versatile than they were in the pioneer era when men like Jewett, Poole, Cutter, Winsor, Green, Spofford, and others bore the young profession to a position of honor. "The business of a librarian is a profession," Poole stated in the report of 1876,[446] and the American Library Association introduced this notion to the public.

At that time it was felt, not without good reasons, that professional education could and should be gained from practical experience, much as the Library of Congress or the Boston Public, for example, still give their assistants in-service training today. Therefore, when Melvil Dewey came out with his plan for professional education in 1879, he met with suspicion, and only the magnetic power of his personality was able to win support for the plan from the conference of 1883 and the senate of Columbia College.[447] In January 1887 the School of Library Economy was opened at Columbia. It was the first library school in the world and the parent of all the American library schools which followed in the next decades. By 1915 the number of library schools had increased to such an extent and their work had become so varied that ten accredited schools felt it advisable to found an Association of American Library Schools on the basis of their curricula and prerequisites. In 1924 the American Library Association founded a special Board of Education for Librarianship, and in the following years it set up minimum standards, curricula and examinations, and three types of schools, viz., graduate (four), undergraduate (two), and junior undergraduate (eight).[448] In a rearrangement of 1933 twenty-six schools were recognized and classified into three types: those not requiring a college education (ten), those requiring four years of college (eleven), and those accepting only students holding a bachelor's degree (five).

Between 1887 and the present day there has been a significant change of thought. The Columbia school wanted to teach library science, i.e., the best, most economical method of selection, purchase, arrangement, cataloguing, indexing, and administration of collections of books, pamphlets, and periodicals.[449] Historical and antiquarian fields were emphasized only as explanatory matter for other fields. In this limitation lay a basic fault of Dewey's school, whose methods led to an overemphasis of the practical side of library work and neglect of intellectual and scholarly training. The rapidly progressing technical nature of library work and the architectural advances before and after 1900 strengthened this tendency even more. In part, library schools assigned undue value to routine and specialization and therefore fell into a certain degree of discredit in academic circles; and this situation was not ameliorated by the heavy female penetration of the profession.[450] The modest standards of the curriculum were not made to attract able workers inspired with a zeal for research, and the value of the degrees and diplomas as reflected in placement and rank did not correspond to expectations.

Criticism of the instructional methods by academicians as well as librarians brought forth a basic report presented by C. C. Williamson to the Carnegie Corporation in 1923. Here was a turning point.[451] Among other things Williamson demanded tightening of entrance requirements and a limitation of professional employees, scientific training (somewhat in the style of Göttingen) in a few qualified schools, closer relationships between these schools and the universities, and the building up of high-ranking faculties. Trends in education for librarianship now emphasize routine less than advanced study. A significant step in this direction came in 1926 with the founding of the Graduate Library School in Chicago with the rank of a faculty of the university, a dean, and full professors.[452] With the aid of the school's organ, the *Library Quarterly,* monographs, and theses there were formulated the bases of a new method of instruction (seminars), indeed, a new philosophy of librarianship, although in a somewhat one-sided manner. It was believed that in order to understand the methods and the work of a library, the librarian himself must have mastered some academic field; that the significance of the library as a "social agency," as a sociological phenomenon, must lie at the core of the instruction; that library science should pursue research problems not so much in the fields of the history of libraries, books, literature, and education as in fields of administration, legislation, finance, social and reader psychology, and sociology.[453] The work of the school is oriented in this direction as well as that of the ancillary Library Institute, at which free lectures and courses are given by university teachers, librarians, and men in public life.[454] There can be no doubt but that the work of the Chicago school and the related one at Columbia have been successful in many respects; but the fact cannot be overlooked that training methods applied in libraries with an old and strong tradition of research such as Harvard, Yale, Michigan, and the Library of Congress are equally good, if not superior. Likewise many research and special libraries must also be recognized as excellent schools of library training.

PROFESSIONAL ORGANIZATION

One of the most outstanding American librarians has passed the retrospective judgment that the development of libraries has been promoted far more by public demand than by the opinions and work of experts, indeed, that there has scarcely been one step forward without running against the denial and the opposition of professional librarians.[455] If this is true, then the American Library Association at all events can make a legitimate claim to having kept pace with progress and with the public during the six decades of its existence. What had been vainly attempted once before in 1853 by men like Poole, Winsor, and Jewett[456] was put through successfully at the Philadelphia conference of 1876: the unification of library workers in one professional organization, the first in the world.[457] At that time the public conception of the needs of libraries was still slight. Accordingly, the constitution of 1877 correctly expressed the purpose of the organization as the promotion of libraries by awakening public interest in the attainment of legal foundations for their support and improvement. Consideration for the approval of public opinion also brought cultural and educational trends to the forefront, and it promoted cooperation with all forces and organizations with similar purposes. Therefore it also appeared to be taken for granted from the very beginning that no purely professional society was to be founded but that the list of members should be expanded to include all who were interested or participated in library work, publishers, bookdealers, educators, and trustees. Professional exclusiveness was all the more distant at that time since there were scarcely any definite characteristics of the library profession, and since one of the principal aims of the group was to create a definite practice of library science by mutual enterprises and exchanges of experience and to give meaning to the conception of librarianship. It was a publisher, Frederick Leypoldt, and a librarian, Melvil Dewey, who realized in the founding of the *Library Journal* (1876) the plan they had both cherished of promoting the interests of libraries as well as of the public by a professional periodical.

Convictions such as those which were brought before the public by the "seer and inspirer," Melvil Dewey, penetrated the American Library Association policy and helped to shape it in the ensuing decades. With the extension of the library movement in the nineties and with the increased numbers of librarians and members, the Association began to split up in groups and sections, beginning with the College and Reference Section in 1889 and the Trustees' Section in 1890, until twelve sections and a constantly growing number of sub-sections, committees, and loosely organized groups gradually came into existence. In addition there were numerous state or regional groups, some of which were linked to the national organization as chapters. Moreover, there were many national associations not connected with the Association but represented within it, such as the Law Libraries (1906), Special Libraries (1909), State Libraries (1889), and Library Commissions (1904). It was an almost confusing number of organizations which overlapped and cut across fields of activity and split up the annual conferences of the Association into countless group meetings. The promotion and administration of the rapidly growing organization, which had 1,000 members in 1900 and has 15,000 today, were not easy; and the increasing strength of the public libraries shifted the weight of the policy in this direction. In addition, the administration of the American Library Association gradually fell into the hands of an executive board, and the general secretariat (1906) dependent on it, while the influence of the authoritative council of 155 members and of the president elected for a term of one year was gradually decreased. At the insistence of the College and Reference Section a reorganization committee was established. It met in 1930 and 1934 and in 1939 presented a comprehensive program for reorganization in the interest of internal integration and compromise between the various interests.[458]

If there was a weakness in this undemocratic development of the Association, there was also strength. Its contribution lay in having prevented disintegration into special groups, in having preserved the unity of librarianship, and in having strengthened professional awareness. It has succeeded in raising the social position of the librarian, although not his modest salary.[459] It has shown itself to be a powerful factor in public affairs and the cultural life of the nation, and it has contributed fundamentally by publication of reference works, monographs, and reading lists, beginning as early as 1886. It has inspired, promoted, and directed interest in all problems of librarianship, and it has initiated and carried out cooperative enterprises. By a wise policy it has been able to maintain contacts with official quarters and national organizations and also to secure necessary grants for its far-flung activities.

CONCLUSION

The history of American libraries goes back to the colonial period, but librarianship as a coherent phenomenon is young; and its principal work has been accomplished only in recent decades. The free initiative of individuals and corporations proved to be one of the strongest factors in building up individual libraries as well as the profession as a whole, and America can thank this circumstance for her public libraries and many of her research libraries. The communities and the state were late in participating in the development of libraries, and then participated only half-heartedly. The federal government did not establish a Library Service Division until January 1, 1938, but it may be considered the beginning of a federal policy for libraries. Just as the local government, librarianship was also thrown back on self-administration and self-support. Many faults but also many virtues have resulted from these historic circumstances. Still lacking are generally applicable legal regulations on financial security, administration, and availability of libraries, and on the preparation, rank, and salaries of the personnel. There are only the beginnings of a national, or even interstate, interlibrary loan system, and the distribution of libraries over the country as a whole and library provision of large regions is still unsatisfactory. But if it is remembered that American librarianship to date lacks the more favorable conditions of libraries in other countries where there is a clear and purposeful state leadership in the cultural and scientific life of the nation, then the accomplishments of American librarians and their organization must be recognized more than ever. A few of these are the improvement of library architecture and administrative practice, establishment of regional and municipal library systems, creation of special and research libraries, and participation in the educational, social, and cultural movements of the age. What is incipient today and perhaps a reality in the near future is the foundation of a national library system.[460]

NOTES

1. There is no general description and history of British librarianship. The article "Libraries" in the *Encyclopaedia Britannica* (in the 11th ed., XVI, 545-77, by J. D. Brown and H. R. Tedder; in the 14th, XVI, 1-25, by Arundell Esdaile, E. A. Baker *et al.*) is very general and only in the 14th ed. gives extensive references to the literature. On the other hand, monographic descriptions of libraries, groups of libraries, librarians, and collectors are very numerous and in part quite valuable. Extremely important material on British library history is contained in the reports of official and corporate commissions which have been appointed to investigate conditions and problems.

   A very good, reliable, and exhaustive bibliography of the pertinent professional literature (not only of Great Britain but also of other countries) is the *Bibliography of Librarianship* (London, Library Association, 1934) compiled by Margaret Burton and M. E. Vosburgh for the Library Association. H. G. T. Cannons' *Bibliography of Library Economy . . . from 1876 to 1920* (Chicago, American Library Assn., 1927) continued by *Library Literature* (1934 to date, covering the period from 1920 to date), is quite complete and contains many items of historical interest; but the dictionary form of *Library Literature* makes it less usable than the selective, conveniently classified arrangement of Burton and Vosburgh. J. D. Brown's *Manual of Library Economy* (4th ed. by W. C. Berwick Sayers, London, Grafton, 1931) gives reviews of literature at the end of individual chapters; and in addition there is bibliographical material in the appendix, "The Librarian's Library" by Richard Wright (pp. 509-25). L. Montagu Harrod compiled "The Librarian's Library" for the 5th ed. of 1937 (pp. 561-91). A selective bibliography for the individual branches of librarianship has appeared since 1902 in the "Syllabus of the Professional Examinations Conducted by the Library Association" in its *Year Book* (1893 to date). *The Year's Work in Librarianship* edited by Esdaile (1929 to date) gives surveys of the progress of research with citations.

   The classical work on library history, Edward Edwards' *Memoirs of Libraries* (2 vols., London, Trübner, 1859; 2d ed. [incomplete], London, 1901), is still a mine of valuable information, even though the bibliographical apparatus is full of lacunae and occasionally even inaccurate. Hereafter this work will be cited as Edwards.

2. J. B. Mullinger, "The Foundation of Libraries," *Cambridge History of English Literature*, IV, 474-97, with extensive bibliography, pp. 621-22; John Leland, *De rebus Britannicis collectanea* (6 vols., edited by Thomas Hearne, Oxonii, e theatro Sheldoniano, 1715; *ed. al.*, 6 vols., Londoni, Richardson, 1770); *idem, Itinerary* (9 vols., edited by Thomas Hearne, Oxford, 1710-12; 2d ed., 9 vols., [in English], Oxford, 1744-45; 3d ed., 9 vols., [in English], Oxford, 1768-69); and Thomas Fuller, *The Church History of Britain* (3 vols., edited by James Nichols, London, Tegg, 1837).

3. 1535: An Act That All Religious Houses Under the Yearly Revenue of £200 Shall

Be Dissolved and Given to the King and His Heirs; 1539: An Act for the Dissolution of All Monasteries and Abbeys (27 Henry VIII, C. 28; 31 Henry VIII, C. 13). Cf. Fuller, *op. cit.*, II, 201 ff., 208.

4. Edwards, I, 357; 2d ed., 187 ff.; and Fuller, *op. cit.*, II, 211-50.

5. John Bale (John Strype, *Life and Acts of Matthew Parker* ₁London, Wyat, 1711₎, pp. 528-29, 538-40) and after him Fuller (*op. cit.*, II, 247-49) report the wanton destruction of libraries and the abuse of books and manuscripts; but Bale's statements may have been exaggerated, since in Continental libraries (Vatican, Leyden, Wolfenbüttel) only a few traces of former property of English cloisters has been found. Cf. Edwards, I, 360-61, and J. W. Clark, *The Care of Books* (Cambridge, University Press, 1901), p. 246 f.

6. H. E. Reynolds, "Our Cathedral Libraries," *Transactions and Proceedings of the Library Association of the United Kingdom*, I (1879), 32-43; and Beriah Botfield, *Notes on the Cathedral Libraries of England* (London, Chiswick Press, 1849).

7. Edwards, I, 365.

8. Concerning Leland see Sidney Lee in *Dictionary of National Biography*, XXXIII, 13-17. Hereafter the *Dictionary of National Biography* will be cited as *D.N.B.* Anthony à Wood, *The Life and Times of Anthony Wood, Antiquary, of Oxford, 1623-1695* (5 vols., collected from his diaries and other papers by Andrew Clark, Oxford, Printed for the Oxford Historical Society, Clarendon Press, 1891-1900), IV, 279-80.

9. Edwards, I, 535-622.

10. J. B. Mullinger, *The University of Cambridge* (3 vols., Cambridge, University Press, 1873), 322-27; W. D. Macray, *Annals of the Bodleian Library, Oxford* (2d ed., Oxford, Clarendon Press, 1890). Hereafter these works will be cited as Mullinger and Macray respectively. Rashdall, *Universities of Europe in the Middle Ages* (3 vols., new ed. by F. M. Powicke and A. B. Emden, Oxford, Clarendon Press, 1936), III, 167, says: "Duke Humphrey's library contained . . . a considerable number of Greek and Latin classics, together with some works of Italian scholars."

11. Mullinger, I, 571, 629.

12. *Ibid.*, p. 541 ff. *et passim;* II, 247 *et passim.*

13. Macray, p. 13.

14. Mullinger, II, 50, 247 (note 3).

15. Thomas Bodley, *Life, Written by Himself* (Chicago, McClurg, 1906; "Literature of Libraries in the Seventeenth and Eighteenth Centuries," no. 3), and *Letters to Thomas James, First Keeper of the Bodleian Library* (edited by G. W. Wheeler, Oxford, Clarendon Press, 1926). Bodley's will is reprinted in *Trecentale Bodleianum* (Oxford, Clarendon Press, 1913), pp. 67-86; the *Life* on pp. 2-20; and the *First Draught of the Statutes of the Publick Library at Oxon* on pp. 29-64. The text of the will may also be found in Macray, pp. 402-18.

16. Bodley, *Letters*, pp. 35, 171, 219.

17. Macray, p. 53.

18. *Ibid.*, pp. 40-41.

19. *Ibid.*, pp. 68-73 (Pembroke), 78-81 (Digby), 83-88 (Laud), 110-23 (Selden).

20. *Ibid.*, p. 31.

21. C. H. Cooper, *Annals of Cambridge* (5 vols., Cambridge, Warwick, 1842-53); and Mullinger.

22. Strype, *op. cit.*, pp. 485-86, 517-23; and H. H. Luard, "A Letter from Bishop Bale to Archbishop Parker," *Cambridge Antiquarian Society Communications*, III (1867), 157-73.

23. Plans for a new building were first proposed in 1614; and in 1640, £8,000 was collected and permission given by Charles I. See Cooper, *op. cit.*, III, 164, 198, 300.

24. *Ibid.*, pp. 397, 405-7, 503.

25. Mullinger, III, 273 *et passim.*

26. Edwards, II, 16 ff.; P. J. Anderson, *Aberdeen University Library* (Aberdeen, University Press, 1914); W. P. Dickson, *The University of Glasgow* (Glasgow, Maclehose, 1888); James Coutts, *A History of the University of Glasgow, 1451 to 1909* (Glasgow, Maclehose, 1909); David Cuthbertson, *The Edinburgh University Library* (Edinburgh, Schulze, 1910); and Alexander Grant, *The Story of the University of Edinburgh During Its First Three Hundred Years* (2 vols., London, Longman, 1884), vol. II.
27. Edwards, II, 45-82.
28. Alexander Gordon, "James Ussher," *D.N.B.*, LVIII, 64-72; and J. Ingram, "Opening Address," *Transactions and Proceedings of the Library Association of the United Kingdom*, VII (1890), 13-24.
29. Edwards, II, 108-60; and G. A. E. Bogeng, *Die grossen Bibliophilen* (3 vols., Leipzig, Seemann, 1922), I, 388 ff. Edwards, *Free Town Libraries* (London, Trübner, 1869), p. 3 ff., counts 306 private libraries from the sixteenth century to 1868. They are divided into 55 lay libraries, 41 clerical libraries, and 202 belonging to scholars and other collectors. Cf. also John Bagford, "Old London Libraries," *Notes and Queries*, 2d ser., XI (1861), 381-84, 401-4, 421-24, 441-45, 461-64.
30. Edwards, I, 416; and G. B. Rawlings, *The British Museum Library* (London, Grafton, 1916), p. 187.
31. Leland, "The Laboriouse Journey and Serche for England's Antiquities, Given of Hym as a New Yeares Gift to King Henry the VIII," reprinted in Hearne's edition of the *Itinerary*, 3d ed., I, xviii-xxiv. Cf. also Lee, *op. cit.*
32. *A Journey Into England in the Year 1598* (translated by Richard Bentley and edited by Horace Walpole, Strawberry Hill, 1757), pp. 30-31.
33. Sir Humphrey Gilbert, "Queene Elizabeth's Academy," *Early English Text Society Publications*, extra ser., vol. VIII (1869); and Edwards, I, 418-19. However, the plan implied less a national library than a library for Archbishop Parker's archaeological society to which it was desired to add the name of the Queen. Cf. Society of Antiquaries, "Introduction: Containing an Historical Account of the Origin and Establishment of the Society of Antiquaries," *Archaeologia: or Miscellaneous Tracts Relating to Antiquity*, I (1770), iii, and Esdaile, "The Preservation of a National Literature," *Library Association Record*, new ser., IV (1926), 216-17.
34. Edwards, *Lives of the Founders of the British Museum, 1570-1870* (London, Trübner, 1870), pp. 153-71.
35. Also the Sedition Act, 14 Charles II, C. 33. Cf. Edwards, II, 584-85.
36. H. L. Bennett, "Thomas Rotherham" (otherwise known as Thomas Scot), *D.N.B.*, XLIX, 301-4; and Mullinger, I, 323. As Chancellor of Cambridge Thomas Scot gave the university's library 200 volumes and must be considered its real founder.
37. W. Roberts, "Some Famous Libraries: 1. The Lambeth Palace Library," *The Bookworm*, I (1888), 69-72; R. A. Rye, *The Student's Guide to the Libraries of London* (3d ed., London, University of London Press, 1927), pp. 34-35; and Edwards, I, 714-25.
38. Mullinger, II, Chapter 3, and his article on "Matthew Parker," *D.N.B.*, XLIII, 254-64; Matthew Parker, *Correspondence of Matthew Parker* (edited for the Parker Society by John Bruce and T. T. Perowne, Cambridge, 1853).
39. See note 5 of this text.
40. *Correspondence*, nos. 99, 221. Flacius Illyricus wrote to Parker on May 22, 1561 that he wanted to send a good agent to England to get manuscripts promised him by the queen a year ago. Parker answered him on July 18, 1563 (date uncertain, perhaps 1566) that it would not be possible for him to hand over the manuscripts, but that he would lend them for one year—perhaps the first example of international interlibrary loan. Cf. also Strype, *op. cit.*, (Appendix, Book II, no. 18, pp. 31-32.)
41. Edwards, I, 714.

42. *Ibid.*, p. 621.
43. Edwards, II, 63-67.
44. Edwards, *Lives*, p. 426 f., and *Free Town Libraries*, pp. 38-40.
45. Edwards, *Lives*, pp. 172-202.
46. Henry Guppy, *The John Rylands Library, Manchester, 1899-1924* (Manchester, Manchester University Press, 1924), p. 93 ff.
47. P. 51 f.
48. See note 29 of this text.
49. For Camden, see E. M. Thompson in *D.N.B.*, VIII, 277-85, and Edwards, *Lives*, pp. 52-53; for Selden, see Edward Fry in *D.N.B.*, LI, 212-24, and Edwards, I, 540-42.
50. Edwards, *Lives*, pp. 48-152.
51. *Ibid.*, p. 134.
52. W. H. Spilsbury, *Lincoln's Inn . . . with an Account of Its Library* (London, Pickering, 1850); Edwards, I, 726-33; and J. M. Rigg, "Matthew Hale," *D.N.B.*, XXIV, 18-24. Hale specified that the books given by him be chained and not be given away or lent for outside use.
53. Edwards, I, 734.
54. Rye, *op. cit.*, p. 20-22; E. M. Borrajo, "The Guildhall Library, Its History and Present Position," *Library Association Record*, X (1908), 381-95; W. S. Saunders, *Guildhall Library: Its Origin and Progress* (London, W. H. O. L. Collingridge, City Press, 1869); and Charles Welch, *The Guildhall Library and Its Work* (London, Library Committee, 1893).
55. A. C. Bickley, "Some Famous Libraries: 4. Sion College Library," *The Bookworm*, I (1888), 265-69.
56. Edwards, I, 623-79; and Albert Nicholson, *The Chetham Hospital and Library* (London, Sherratt and Hughes, 1910).
57. Bodley left his library £7000, and other sums went to Merton and other colleges. The relatives of his wife, who had brought him a fortune, ended rather impecuniously. As late as 1712 their descendants were receiving a pension of a few pounds from the university. See Macray, pp. 48-49.
58. *Ibid.*, p. 224. At the same time the year 1735 signalled "the Century of Great Donations" (Falconer Madan, *The Bodleian Library at Oxford* [London, Duckworth, 1919], p. 28).
59. Cooper, *op. cit.*, III, 397, 405-7, 503. The appropriation was for necessary expenses involved in transporting the library of Archbishop Bancroft from Lambeth to Cambridge and housing it. It was not an endowment to provide a steady income.
60. John Power, "Evidence," pp. 50-60, in Gt. Brit., Commission on the State, Discipline, Studies, and Revenues of the University and Colleges in Cambridge, *Report . . . Evidence, Appendix, and Index* (2 pts., London, 1852-53). This endowment yielded £250 in 1852. Rustat was actually the first to give a money endowment to the library (Mullinger, III, 95).
61. Fuller, *op. cit.*, II, 512; Strype, *op. cit.*, pp. 517-23; and Mullinger, II, 247.
62. Edwards, II, 16-44.
63. See p. 10.
64. Macray, p. 157.
65. The old university library owned about 500 books in 1475. See Mullinger, II, 343-44.
66. Edwards, I, 714-25.
67. *Ibid.*, pp. 596-97.
68. *Ibid.*, pp. 455-59.
69. *Trecentale Bodleianum*, pp. 27-64: "The First Draft of the Statutes . . . the Basis of the First Latin Statutes of 1610." Cf. Bodley, *Letters*, pp. 35, 171, 219.
70. Mullinger, II, 343-44.
71. Edwards, II, 23-24.

72. The conditions of the will are reprinted in Edwards, I, 617-18.
73. Macray, pp. 99-100. Nevertheless, the intention was fulfilled, for soon after Selden's death the greater part of his library went to the Bodleian.
74. Edwards, I, 694.
75. Bogeng, *op. cit.*, I, 425 ff.
76. Edwards, II, 747 ff; and W. R. B. Prideaux, "Library Economy in the Sixteenth Century," *Library Association Record*, XI (1901), 152-74.
77. Bodley, *Letters*, pp. 96-99 *et passim;* and J. W. Spargo, "Some Reference Books of the Sixteenth and Seventeenth Centuries: A Finding List," *Papers of the Bibliographical Society of America*, XXXI (1937), 133-75.
78. The librarian, Thomas Hyde, had planned to work on this catalogue two or three years; but he had to spend six years on the compilation alone and two more in having it set up in type. Cf. Macray, pp. 139-40.
79. The first catalogues of 1425 and 1473 have been preserved. The latter contained 330 books and listed them according to their locations. (Mullinger, I, 323).
80. W. P. Dickson, "The Glasgow University Library: Its Growth by Donations," *The Library*, VIII (1898), 381-93.
81. In Duke Humphrey's day the librarian was Adam Kirkebote, who was followed by a certain Fletcher in 1527 and by Humphrey Bunford in 1543 (Macray, p. 12).
82. Bodley had scheduled his librarian for six hours of service. James, moreover, called these hours shackles and said of Richard de Bury: "vixit in illo aureo seculo cum illis priscis et bonis hominibus" (Mullinger, I, 205, note 2).
83. The first librarian in the sixteenth century was William James, a nephew of Thomas James. His honorarium was all of £10 (Mullinger, II, 343). See D. S. Margoliouth, "Abraham Wheelocke," *D.N.B.*, LX, 443-44; and Norman Moore, "William Moore," *ibid.*, XXXVIII, 386.
84. Thompson Cooper, "Stephen Batman," *D.N.B.*, III, 414.
85. See Edwards, *Lives*, 142-44, on Dr. Smith and William Hanbury. During Bentley's nominal directorship David Casley functioned as keeper (J. H. Monk, *The Life of Richard Bentley* [London, Rivington, 1830], pp. 42, 451).
86. Bulstrode Whitelocke, *Memorials of English Affairs* (new ed., London, Printed for J. Tonson, 1732), pp. 415-16.
87. For John Dury (also spelled Durie) see biography by J. Westby-Gibson in *D.N.B.*, XVI, 261-63; Dury, *The Reformed Librarie-Keeper* (Chicago, McClurg, 1906; "Literature of Libraries in the Seventeenth and Eighteenth Centuries," no. 2) with a biographical sketch by Ruth Sheppard Granniss; Richard Garnett, "Librarianship in the Seventeenth Century," pp. 175-90, in his *Essays in Librarianship and Bibliography* (London, Allen, 1899). Whitelocke calls Dury "a German by birth, and a great traveller and friend to the Parliament." He probably confused him with Samuel Hartlib, Dury's friend from Elbing and London, for Dury was of Scottish descent. Dury died in Kassel in 1680 after spending an unstable life as a wanderer.
88. London, 1650.
89. J. D. Duff, "Scholars and Antiquaries, I. Bentley and Classical Scholarship," *Cambridge History of English Literature*, IX, 368-82; H. G. Aldis, "Scholars and Antiquaries, II. Antiquaries," *ibid.*, 382-400; and J. J. Adamson, "Education," *ibid.*, 425-62.
90. *Oxford in 1710; from the Travels of Zacharias Conrad Uffenbach* (edited by W. H. and W. J. C. Quarrell, Oxford, Blackwell, 1928). Cf. also Predeek, "Bibliotheksbesuche eines gelehrten Reisenden im Anfang des 18. Jahrhunderts," *Zentralblatt für Bibliothekswesen*, XLV (1928), 221-65, 342-54, 393-407.
91. See Monk, *op. cit.*, p. 100 ff.
92. *Memoirs,* (edited by George Birkbeck, London, Methuen, 1900), p. 49 ff.
93. *Edinburgh Review*, XI (1808), 370-90 (*"Letters from England. By Don Manuel*

Alvarez Espriella. Translated from the Spanish. 3 vol. London, Longman & Co. 1807.").

94. Martha Ornstein, *The Rôle of Scientific Societies in the Seventeenth Century* (Chicago, University of Chicago Press, 1928); A. E. Shipley, "The Progress of Science," *Cambridge History of English Literature,* VIII, 399-420; Adamson, *op. cit.;* and Archibald Clarke, "The Work of Academies of Literature and Their Connection with Libraries," *Library Association Record,* I (1899), 286-93.

95. Harold Routh, "Steele and Addison," *Cambridge History of English Literature,* IX, 29-72; and Edward Bensly, "Pope," *ibid.,* pp. 73-100.

96. Macray, pp. 233-47 (Rawlinson), 225-28 (Clarendon).

97. *Ibid.,* p. 347.

98. Edwards, "Appendix," p. 278, in Gt. Brit., Parliament, House of Commons, Select Committee on Public Libraries, *Report . . . Together with the Proceedings of the Committee, Minutes of Evidence* (London, Hansard, 1849).

99. James Boswell, *The Life of Samuel Johnson* (3 vols., edited by Mowbray Morris, London, Macmillan, 1900), I, 397.

100. Macray, p. 276.

101. The real work on the catalogue was done by Hearne (Macray, pp. 213-14). During the period 1859-78 a new catalogue based on the method of British Museum catalogue was begun: all titles were transcribed, duplicated in two to five copies, two of each mounted, put in alphabetical order, and bound.

102. Edwards, II, 12-13.

103. Moore's library, famous all over Europe was offered to the Earl of Oxford in 1714 for £8,000; but it was actually bought for 6,000 guineas by George I, who was persuaded by Lord Townsend to give it to Cambridge (Edwards, I, 596-97).

104. In 1745-51 the Parliament gave almost £10,000, and George II gave £3,000 more. In 1835 a subscription fund of £21,000 made possible a further addition *(ibid.,* p. 599).

105. Power, *op. cit.,* p. 51.

106. Conyers Middleton, *Bibliothecae Cantabrigiensis ordinandae methodus quaedam* (Cantabrigiae, 1723); cf. Edwards, II, 779-81. The classification was made to order for Moore's library. The tract subjected Middleton to a prosecution for libel and a sentence to pay £50 because of a remark in the foreword which offended Bentley *(ibid.,* p. 780, note 2, and Monk, *op. cit.,* pp. 490-93).

107. Edwards, I, 606-9; and Robert Sinker, *The Library of Trinity College, Cambridge* (London, Bell, 1891).

108. Edwards, I, 614-19, and Predeek, *op. cit.,* pp. 246-47.

109. R. C. B. Partridge, *History of the Legal Deposit of Books Throughout the British Empire* (London, Library Association, 1938). Charles II issued the first depository legislation in 1662. It specified delivery of one copy each to the Royal Library, Oxford, and Cambridge. A new and more comprehensive law was issued by Queen Anne in 1709. It specified delivery of nine copies, two to the English university libraries, four to the Scottish university libraries, and one each to the Advocates' Library, the Royal Library and Sion College. George III expanded it to include Trinity College in Dublin, and during the reign of William IV, Sion College surrendered its rights for £363. It was also proposed on many occasions that Oxford, Cambridge, and the Scottish universities surrender their rights, but these proposals were declined for Oxford and Cambridge (Cooper, *op. cit.,* V, 85).

110. Edwards, II, 30-39.

111. *Ibid.,* 46-63.

112. G. B. Rawlings, *The British Museum Library* (London, Grafton, 1916), "Select Bibliography," pp. 221-23; and Robert Cowtan, *Memories of the British Museum* (London, Bentley, 1872). Esdaile, *National Libraries* (London, Grafton, 1934), p. 3 ff., gives a good orientation and excellent description with the most important

references; cf. also his "The Preservation of a National Literature," *loc. cit.* Most important for the history of the foundation is Edwards, I, 415-49. See also Edwards, *Lives;* and L. A. Fagan, *Life of Sir Anthony Panizzi* (2d ed., 2 vols., London, Remington, 1880).

113. Rawlings, *op. cit.*, pp. 221-23. Edwards, I, 421, calls Bentley "the most eminent man who ever held an office." Bentley bought the office from a certain Thynne for an annual rent of £120 (Monk, *op. cit.*, pp. 42, 56, 73).

114. Richard Bentley, *A Proposal for Building a Royal Library, and Establishing It by Act of Parliament* (London, n.d.), a broadside (Edwards, I, 422, note 1).

115. Monk, *op. cit.*, p. 577; and Gt. Brit., Parliament, House of Commons, Committee on the Cottonian Library, *A Report from the Committee Appointed to View the Cottonian Library* (London, Printed for R. Williamson and W. Bowyer, 1732).

116. Edwards, I, 434-39, and *Lives*, p. 134. At the death of Robert Harley the library amounted to 6,000 volumes of manuscripts, 14,000 charters and 500 "rolls." Edward, second Earl of Oxford, increased it to 8,000 volumes of manuscripts, 41,000 prints, 50,000 volumes of printed books, and 400,000 pamphlets.

117. Edwards, I, 439-43; and Rawlings, *op. cit.*, pp. 47-54 (Sloane), pp. 19-45 (Cottonian Library).

118. By the act of incorporation (Edwards, I, 442) the institution received the name British Museum. Cf. also Rawlings, *op. cit.*, pp. 51-52.

119. For the earlier government see Gt. Brit., Parliament, House of Commons, Select Committee on the Condition, Management and Affairs of the British Museum, *Report . . . Together with Minutes of Evidence, Appendix and Index* (London, 1835-36).

120. The three principal trustees (ex officio) were the archbishop of Canterbury, the lord chancellor, and the speaker of the House of Commons. The following families were represented: Sloane (two), Cotton (two), Harley (two), Townley (one), Elgin (one), Knight (one), all up to the present day. In addition there was one trustee to represent the king. Among others, trustees named by the king included the president of the Royal Society of Arts and the president of the Royal Academy. Cf. also Rawlings, *op. cit.*, appendix II, pp. 208-9.

121. See the amusing description of the trustees by Horace Walpole in a letter of February 1753, and Edwards, *Lives*, pp. 322-31.

122. The succession of early librarians was as follows: Dr. Gowin Knight, 1757-72; Dr. Matthew Maty, 1772-76; Dr. Charles Morton, 1776-99; Joseph Planta, 1799-1827; and Henry Ellis, 1827-56.

123. Gt. Brit., Parliament, House of Commons, Select Committee on the Condition, Management and Affairs of the British Museum, *op. cit.;* Edwards, *Remarks on the Minutes of Evidence Taken Before the Select Committee* (2d ed., London, 1836); and Sir Nicholas Harris Nicolas, *Observations on the State of Historical Literature* (London, Pickering, 1830).

124. Also called the King's Tracts (Edwards, *Lives*, pp. 21-22).

125. Edwards, I, 524-25, and *Lives*, pp. 422-35.

126. T. F. Dibdin, *A Bibliographical, Antiquarian and Picturesque Tour in France and Germany* (2d ed., 3 vols., London, 1829), III, 157-59.

127. B. D. Jackson, "Joseph Banks," *D.N.B.*, III, 129-33; Jonas Dryander, *Catalogus bibliotecae historico-naturalis Josephi Banks* (5 vols., Londoni, typis G. Bulmer, 1796-1800); G. S. Boulges, "Jonas Dryander," *D.N.B.*, XVI, 64.

128. Edwards, I, 115-16; and Fagan, *op. cit.*, I, 115-16. At the death of George III, £200,000 was offered for the library, which at that time numbered 34,000 items.

129. Edwards, *Lives*, pp. 337-41; Rawlings, *op. cit.*, p. 60 ff.; and G. F. A. Wendeborn, *A View of England Towards the Close of the Eighteenth Century* (Dublin, Printed by W. Sleater for P. Wogan, 1791).

130. Similar complaints concerning the undue haste of the tours were uttered as late

as 1837 ("The British Museum," *Mechanics Magazine*, XXVII [1837], 16).

131. When Planta took office, there were still less than 200 patrons a day, but by 1830 Ellis could report an annual count of almost 100,000. In 1850 it was nearly 1,000,000.

132. Edwards, *Lives*, p. 583 ff.; Fagan, *op. cit.*, I, 105-6; Rawlings, *op. cit.*, pp. 66-67, 81 ff. Moving was executed in 1838-39, during which period it was possible for 5 per cent of the books to remain in use.

133. F. J. Teggart, "Library Literature in England and the United States During the Nineteenth Century," *Library Journal*, XXVI (1901), 257-61, should be added to the general bibliographies for the nineteenth century.

134. Complaints were made against the narrowness of the reading room, the bad air ("Museum-headache!"), the poor catalogues, the lacunae in the holdings, and the insufficient appropriations.

135. The critic was Sir Nicholas Harris Nicolas (biography by W. P. Courtney, *D.N.B.*, XLI, 41-44) and the employee a certain Millard. See Fagan, *op. cit.*, I, 153; and Edwards, *Lives*, pp. 536, 541.

136. The commission, which was headed by S. Estcourt, formulated in its final report eighteen proposals for reorganization, among them reduction of the number of trustees, better departmentalization, strengthening of the position of the principal librarian and the divisional chiefs, and better salaries.

137. For Panizzi's role and the reports of the second commission of 1847-49 see Predeek, "Antonio Panizzi und der alphabetische Katalog des Britischen Museums," in *Festschrift Georg Leyh* (Leipzig, Harrassowitz, 1937), pp. 257-82, with pertinent references. English abridgement in *Library Association Record*, XXXIX (1937), 515-20, 579-82, 622-26.

138. In 1836 Edwards published a tract on the lacunae in the British Museum, especially in the field of German literature: *Remarks on the "Minutes of Evidence" Taken Before the Select Committee on the British Museum* (2d ed., London, Compton and Ritchie, Printers, 1839); original edition of 1836 published under title *A Letter to Benjamin Hawes; Being Strictures on the "Minutes of Evidence. . . ."* Cf. also Thomas Greenwood, *Edward Edwards* (London, Scott, 1902), pp. 9, 223.

139. Annual appropriations were raised from the average of £1,135 for the preceding twenty years to £3,443.

140. Henry Stevens, "Twenty Years' Reminiscences of Panizzi and the British Museum, 1845-1865," *Transactions and Proceedings of the Library Association of the United Kingdom*, VII (1890), 117-24.

141. Predeek, "Antonio Panizzi und der alphabetische Katalog des Britischen Museums," *loc. cit.*, p. 273, note 1.

142. Average annual accessions were about 10,000 volumes. See British Museum, *List of Additions Made to the Collections in the British Museum* for 1831-35, 1836-38, 1839-1910, 1911-15, 1916-20 (London, 1833 to 1933).

143. Edwards, I, 494-505, 526-29, and *Lives*, p. 608 ff.

144. Edwards, I, 490-93, and *Lives*, p. 670 ff. J. T. Payne and Henry Foss, comps., *Biblioteca Grenvilliana* (3 vols., London, Printed by W. Nicol, 1842-72).

145. Gt. Brit., Commissioners Appointed to Inquire into the Constitution and Government of the British Museum, *Report . . . with Minutes of Evidence* (London, Printed by W. Clowes and Sons for H. M. Stationery Off., 1850).

146. Predeek, "Antonio Panizzi und der alphabetische Katalog des Britischen Museums," *loc. cit.*, p. 275 ff.

147. W. E. A. Axon, "Is a Printed Catalog of the British Museum Practicable?" *Transactions and Proceedings of the Library Association of the United Kingdom*, I (1879) 65-67; Garnett, "The Printing of the British Museum Catalogue," in his *Essays in Librarianship and Bibliography*, pp. 67-87; *idem*, "Public Libraries and Their Catalogues," *ibid.*, pp. 32-66; *idem*, "The Past, Present, and Future of the British

Museum Catalogue," *ibid.*, pp. 87-108; G. K. Fortescue, "The British Museum Catalogue and the Compilation of the General Catalogue of Printed Books," *Library Association Record*, III (1901), 435-49; Rawlings, *op. cit.*, p. 142 ff.; and Edwards, II, 850-68.

148. Karl Dziatzko, "Die Bibliothek und Lesesaal des Britischen Museums," *Preussische Jahrbücher*, XLVIII (1881), 346-76.

149. Fortescue applied to the catalogue the saying of Cardinal Maury about his services, "When I consider, 'No,' when I compare, 'Yes,' " *(op. cit.*, p. 141).

150. Fagan, *op. cit.*, I, 338 ff.; Edwards, I, 513-34, and *Lives*, p. 583 ff. (describes the reading room as well as later expansions, including sketches); Dziatzko, *op. cit.*; W. Hosking, *Some Remarks upon the Recent Addition of a Reading-Room to the British Museum* (London, 1848); "Professor Hosking's Project," *The Builder*, VIII (1850), 295-96 (with plan); and P.P.C.R., "The New Building at the British Museum," *Mechanics Magazine*, XXVI (1837), 454-59 (plan by Watts).

151. The classification drawn up by Watts, Winter Jones, and Panizzi after 1838 followed the then customary scheme of dividing the sciences according to logical-philosophical viewpoints. Each of the fifteen principal classes (with about 500 subdivisions altogether) contained an aggregate of 1,000 shelves. Books were numbered continuously within the groups, and the earlier fixed location was given up. By 1877 the number of subdivisions had reached 700. See T. H. Horne, *Outlines for the Classification of a Library; Respectfully Submitted to the Consideration of the Trustees of the British Museum* (London, Printed by G. Woodfall, 1825); Garnett, "On the System of Classifying Books in the British Museum," *Essays in Librarianship and Bibliography*, pp. 210-24; J. Winter Jones, "Inaugural Address" (to the Library Conference, 1877), *Library Journal*, II (1877), 99-119; Predeek, *Das moderne englische Bibliothekswesen* (Leipzig, Harrassowitz, 1933; *Zentralblatt für Bibliothekswesen*, "Beiheft," no. 66).

152. Esdaile, *National Libraries*, pp. 5-12.

153. *Ibid.*, pp. 4-5.

154. Garnett, "The Past, Present, and the Future of the British Museum Catalogue," *loc. cit.*

155. Lord (George N.) Curzon, *Principles and Methods of University Reform* (Oxford, Clarendon Press, 1909), "Introduction."

156. Gt. Brit., University Grants Committee, *Returns from Universities and University Colleges in Receipt of Treasury Grant* (London, 1921 to date; the *Returns* for 1919/1920 are issued in the series of *Papers by Command*, cmd. 1263).

157. Gt. Brit., Commission on the State, Discipline, Studies and Revenues of the University and Colleges of Oxford, *Report . . . Evidence, Appendix and Index* (2 pts., London, 1852-53); Edwards, I, 553-73.

158. Macray, pp. 371-74.

159. *Ibid.*, pp. 386-87.

160. Oxford University, Commission Appointed by the Congregation of the University, *Library Provision in Oxford* (Oxford, Clarendon Press, 1931).

161. E. C. Thomas, "The Libraries of Oxford, and the Use of College Libraries," *Transactions and Proceedings of the Library Association of the United Kingdom*, I (1879), 24-28; and C. H. Robarts, "University Libraries as National Institutions," *Library Journal*, II (1877), 129-40.

162. Oxford University, Commission Appointed by the Congregation of the University, *op. cit.*

163. Gt. Brit., Commission on the State, Discipline, and Revenues of the University and Colleges in Cambridge, *op. cit.*, pp. 127-32 (the public library), 133-34 (the college libraries), 50-60 (Power, *op. cit.*); and Edwards, I, 600 ff.

164. Predeek, *Das moderne englische Bibliothekswesen*, p. 108.

165. G. W. Prothero, "Henry Bradshaw," *D.N.B.*, XXII (supp.), 251-59; Henry Brad-

shaw, *Collected Papers* (Cambridge, University Press, 1889); Henry Bradshaw, "Some Account of the Organisation of the Cambridge University Library," *Transactions and Proceedings of the Library Association of the United Kingdom,* V (1884), 229-37; G. W. Prothero, *A Memoir of Henry Bradshaw* (London, Paul, 1888); C. F. Newcombe, "Some Aspects of the Work of Henry Bradshaw," *Library Association Record,* VII (1905), 392-403.

166. Prothero, *A Memoir of Henry Bradshaw,* p. 314.

167. *Ibid.,* p. 373 ff.

168. Mullinger and Cloudesley Brereton, "Universities. Great Britain and Ireland. Modern Times," *Encyclopaedia Britannica,* 14th ed., XXII, 872-74.

169. Rye, *op. cit.,* pp. 62-67.

170. R. W. Chambers, "The Library of the University College of London," *Library Association Record,* XI (1909), 350-58.

171. Rye, *op. cit.,* pp. 67, 200-1.

172. *Ibid.,* pp. 298-300.

173. Mullinger and Brereton, *op. cit.;* and R. Offor, "University Libraries During the Reign" (of George V), *Library Association Record,* 4th ser., II (1935), 220-21. Cf. also Gt. Brit., Universities Grants Committee, *op. cit.,* 1919, 1921, 1925, 1930.

174. C. R. Weld, *A History of the Royal Society, with Memoirs of the Presidents* (2 vols., London, Parker, 1848); Edwards, II, 89-92; and Rye, *op. cit.,* pp. 37, note 1, and 409-10.

175. Clark, *op. cit.*

176. Edwards, II, 72-76; Esdaile, *National Libraries,* pp. 55-60; and Guthrie Vine, "The National Library of Ireland," *Library Association Record,* IV (1902), 92-109.

177. Edwards, II, 3-15, and W. K. Dickson, "The National Library of Scotland," in Library Association, *Proceedings of the Fiftieth Anniversary Conference* (London, Library Association, 1928), pp. 34-44; also appeared in *Library Journal,* LII (1927), 1119-23.

178. J. H. Burton, *Life and Correspondence of David Hume* (2 vols., Edinburgh, Tait, 1846), I, 372.

179. H. W. Meikle, "The National Library of Scotland; Proposed New Buildings," *Library Association Record,* XXXIX (1937), 13-15; and Esdaile, *National Libraries,* pp. 36-48.

180. W. L. Davis, "The National Library of Wales," *Library Association Record,* XXXIX (1937), 375-78; Esdaile, *National Libraries,* pp. 48-55; H. R. Tedder, *The National Library of Wales* (Aberdeen, University Press, 1911).

181. Edwards, II, 131-32; Bogeng, *op. cit.,* I, 438-39 (Roxburghe), 440-42 (Beckford), 453-54 (Heber); "Richard Heber," *Gentleman's Magazine,* new ser., I (1834), 105-9 (Bibliotheca Heberiana); T. F. Dibdin, *Bibliomania* (2d ed., London, Longman, 1811), pp. 171-83.

182. C. A. Cutter, *Expansive Classification* (Boston, Author, 1891-93).

183. Guppy, *op. cit.,* p. 94; and Bogeng, *op. cit.,* I, 450-51.

184. Edwards, II, 147-51; Guppy, *op. cit.;* Charles Bruce, "The Althorp Library," *Transactions and Proceedings of the Library Association of the United Kingdom,* VII (1890), 51-60.

185. Edwards, II, 147-51; Guppy, *op. cit.; Bulletin of the John Rylands Library,* vol. I (1923) to date.

186. C. T. Wright, *The London Library; a Sketch of Its History and Administration* (London, London Library, 1926); Rye, *op. cit.,* pp. 179-80; Frederic Harrison, ed., *Carlyle and the London Library* (London, Chapman and Hall, 1907).

187. Wilhelm Dibelius, *England* (2 vols., 6th ed. by Paul Meissner, Stuttgart, Deutsche Verlags-Anstalt, 1931), II, 148 ff., 174 ff. Rather harsh and scarcely pertinent for this generality is the statement of Clarke, *op. cit.,* 286: "The country squire would not, and the artisan and labourer could not read. The bookloving public

was confined to a comparatively narrow circle of the aristocracy and the middle classes." But as late as the parliamentary debate on the library law of 1850 Colonel Sibthorp, one of its most violent opponents, declared ". . . he did not like reading at all and hated it when at Oxford (!)" (John Minto, *A History of the Public Library Movement in Great Britain and Ireland* ₍London, Allen, 1932₎, p. 83).

188. *Ibid.*, p. 24 ff., and Edwards, I, 752-62.

189. James Kirkwood, *Two Tracts on the Founding and Maintaining of Public Libraries in Scotland* (Chicago, McClurg, 1906, "Literature of Libraries in the Seventeenth and Eighteenth Centuries," no. 4). The first of the two tracts is "An Overture for Establishing of Bibliothecks in Every Paroch Throughout This Kingdom," pp. 17-58.

190. In 1708 Parliament had passed a law entitled "An Act for the Better Preservation of Parochial Libraries in That Part of Great Britain Called England."

191. Gt. Brit., Commission on the Condition of Cathedral and Collegiate Churches in England and Wales, *Report* (4 pts., London, 1854-55).

192. Edwards, I, 762-68; Edwards, *Free Town Libraries*, pp. 8-13; and George Smith, "Dr. Thomas Bray," *Library Association Record*, XII (1910), 242-60.

193. Edwards, II, 63-86.

194. J. G. Fitch, "Joseph Lancaster," *D.N.B.*, XXXII, 39-42; G. P. Macdonell, "Andrew Bell," *D.N.B.*, IV, 149-50; and "Public Libraries," *North British Review*, XV (1851), 160-84.

195. Samuel Brown, Jr., *Some Account of Itinerating Libraries and Their Founder* (Edinburgh, Blackwood, 1856); and Minto, *op. cit.*, pp. 40-46.

196. There were small collections in the vicinity of Martin-in-the-Fields and in Whitcomb Street established by Rector Mackenzie and his curator Brereton (cf. "Public Libraries," *loc. cit.* note 194, *supra*).

197. H. T. Wood, "George Birkbeck," *D.N.B.*, V, 80-81; and James Hole, *Essay on the History and Management of Literary, Scientific, and Mechanics Institutions* (London, Longman, 1853).

198. Edwards, *Free Town Libraries;* Thomas Greenwood, *Public Libraries, A History of the Movement* (4th ed., London, Cassell, 1894); J. J. Ogle, *The Free Library, Its History and Present Condition* (London, Allen, 1897); and Greenwood, *Edward Edwards, The Chief Pioneer of Municipal Public Libraries* (London, Scott, 1902).

199. Edwards had urged before the commission of 1847-49 that a lending branch be attached to the British Museum. Panizzi also had expressed himself in favor of at least one public library in London in 1836. See Edwards, "A Statistical View of the Principal Public Libraries in Europe and the United States of North America," *Journal of the Royal Statistical Society of London*, XI (1848), 250-81. A similar proposal was discussed by P.P.C.R., "The British Museum and Provincial Institutions," *Mechanics Magazine*, XXV (1836), 74-78.

200. G. C. Boase, "William Ewart," *D.N.B.*, XVIII, 91-92; Axon, "Joseph Brotherton," *D.N.B.*, VI, 446; B. H. Mullen, "Salford and the Inauguration of Public Free Libraries: A Contribution to the History of Free Libraries," *Library Association Record*, II (1900), 183-89; J. W. Southern, "Municipal Libraries and Their Development," *Library Association Record*, I, 607-18; and Ogle, *op. cit.*

201. Gt. Brit. Parliament, House of Commons, Select Committee on Public Libraries, *op. cit.;* Edwards, I, 772-92, II, 989-1028; Garnett, "To the Memory of Edward Edwards, the Pioneer of the Public Library Movement," *Library Association Record*, IV (1902), 1-9.

202. The "Bill for Enabling Town Councils to Establish Public Libraries and Museums" was passed by 118 to 110 and received royal approval on August 8, 1850. The designation "free" was omitted in order to avoid the impression that the law was passed only for the benefit of the poorer classes. References to the easily accessible libraries of eighteenth- and nineteenth-century Germany played a part in

the arguments for the law. Ewart pointed out Schiller among others as one who had a constant opportunity to use the libraries of Jena and Weimar; and he added the thought that had Shakespeare been an attorney's clerk in Oxford, he would not have had an opportunity to use the Bodleian(!).

203. Edwards, II, 44 (Scotland), I, 829-33 (Ireland).

204. Southern, *op. cit.*, p. 613.

205. Gt. Brit., Board of Education, Public Libraries Committee, *Report on Public Libraries in England and Wales* (London, H. M. Stationery Off., 1927), pp. 235-40, gives a complete list of the adoptions of law from 1850 to 1926.

206. For the development of library legislation, see among others G. F. Chambers and H. W. Fovargue, *The Law Relating to Public Libraries and Museums and Literary and Scientific Institutions* (4th ed., London, Knight, 1899). A compressed survey is also contained in Gt. Brit., Board of Education, Public Libraries Committee, *op. cit.*, Chapter I.

207. See J. J. Ogle and H. W. Fovargue, *Public Library Legislation; Being the Law Relating to Public Libraries and Technical Education, and All Statutes Directly or Indirectly Affecting Libraries, Museums, Art Galleries, etc., in England, Ireland and Scotland* (London, Simpson, Marshall, Hamilton, Kent, 1893, "Library Association Series," no. 2). Ogle was the librarian of the free public library at Boothe and Fovargue the town clerk of Eastbourne.

208. Rye, *op. cit.*, pp. 68-71.

209. In 1880 Birmingham and Preston had levied higher taxes and then put the restriction aside completely. A law aimed at this purpose had been drawn up by Ballinger, Birmingham, and repeatedly put before Parliament, only to be rejected upon the outbreak of war in 1914. See Minto, *op. cit.*, pp. 127-29.

210. 9 and 10 George V, C. 13. See Gt. Brit., Board of Education, Public Libraries Committee, *op. cit.*, pp. 21-23. In 1920 Scotland and Ireland adopted the law with a minimum of a halfpenny, and in Northern Ireland the limit was set at two pence (1925).

211. According to the report of 1927 which covered 400 library districts in England and Wales, urban communities appropriated between four pence and one shilling, rural communities about nine pence per person. Average income of the public library was about £5,000. More than a hundred libraries had less than £100; and about sixteen libraries with more than 100,000 volumes could show total expenditures of £12,000-£24,000, while three great libraries with over 400,000 volumes spent over £50,000. Nevertheless, only 26 per cent of expenditures went for acquisition and binding, 29 per cent to capital and other expenditures, and 44 per cent went to salaries. See J. M. Mitchell, "Library Budgets," *Library Association Record*, 3d ser., II (1932), 298-304.

212. J. D. Brown, *Manual of Library Economy* (4th ed.); E. A. Baker, *The Public Library* (London, Grafton, 1923); and *idem*, ed., *The Uses of Libraries* (2d ed., London, University of London Press, 1930). Greenwood, *Public Libraries, a History of the Movement* (4th ed.) covers the older period (1850-80) in the same way that Brown covers the more recent one; and the report of 1927 contains a mine of information on the subject. Cf. also Predeek, *Das moderne englische Bibliothekswesen*.

213. Edwards, *Free Town Library*, p. 61 ff.; Greenwood, *Edward Edwards*, p. 107 ff.; C. W. Sutton, "Some of the Institutions of Manchester and Salford," *Library Association Record*, I (1899), 550-63; and W. R. Credland, *The Manchester Public Free Libraries; a History and Description and Guide to Their Contents and Use* (Manchester, Public Free Libraries Co., 1899).

214. In October 1858 Edwards was forced to resign by the town council of Manchester, and it must be said that he was not wholly without blame. From that time on he embarked on an ascetic wandering career, full of tireless, fruitful work. On Feb-

ruary 10, 1886 he died in Niton, Isle of Wight. See Greenwood, *Edward Edwards*, "Introduction," pp. 2, 119-20, 210 ff., and "Appendix," pp. 223-30 (list of Edwards' publications, eighty in all).

215. A. C. Shaw, *The Birmingham Free Libraries* (Aberdeen, University Press, 1902), and Peter Cowell, *Liverpool Public Libraries; a History of Fifty Years* (Liverpool, Free Public Library, 1903).

216. John Warner, *Reference Library Methods* (London, Grafton, 1928), p. 189 ff.

217. Gt. Brit., Board of Education, Public Libraries Committee, *op. cit.*, pp. 174-80, and Joint Committee of the Library Association and the British Institute of Adult Education, *The Public Libraries and Adult Education; an Interim Memorandum on Co-operation Between Public Libraries and Bodies Concerned with Adult Education* (London, Cole, 1923).

218. Dibelius, *op. cit.*, II, 123 ff., 165 ff.

219. Stanley Jast, *The Planning of a Great Library* (London, Libraco, 1927), p. 5.

220. Edwards, *Free Town Libraries*, p. 61 ff.

221. The first to urge open access was J. D. Brown, "A Plea for Liberty to Readers to Help Themselves," *The Library*, IV (1892), 302-5. It was first introduced in the Clerkenwell Public Library. See also Brown, *Manual of Library Economy* (1st ed., 1903, pp. 445-68; 4th ed., p. 10).

222. "Annals of the Library Association," *Library Association Year Book*, 1939, p. 38, gives the following note under the date of October 18, 1894: "Mr. Charles Welch, in a paper on *The Public Library Movement in London*, stated that London libraries were not carrying out the clear intentions of the legislation because from 75 to 80 per cent of the books issued were works of fiction. This paper was the earliest manifestation of the fiction controversy."

223. In 1879 the Library Association adopted a resolution placing a restriction on fiction. See Gt. Brit., Board of Education, Public Libraries Committee, *op. cit.*, pp. 62-64, 251.

224. *Ibid.*, p. 141; Association of Special Libraries and Information Bureaux, *ASLIB Directory: A Guide to the Sources of Specialized Information in Great Britain and Ireland* (edited by G. F. Barwick, London, Oxford University Press, 1928), p. 252.

225. See Rye, *op. cit.*

226. *Ibid.*, pp. 266-78.

227. *Ibid.*, pp. 384-85.

228. *Ibid.*, pp. 170-71 (Athenaeum), pp. 180-81 (Reform Club).

229. *Ibid.*, pp. 407-9; Edwards, *Free Town Libraries*, p. 178 ff.; and H. P. Spratt, *Libraries for Scientific Research in Europe and America* (London, Grafton, 1936), pp. 27, 38 (good summary).

230. *Ibid.*, *passim*. Other technical libraries of London are also discussed here.

231. Predeek, *Das moderne englische Bibliothekswesen*, p. 35.

232. Frederick Bradshaw, "Armstrong College Library," *Library Association Record*, new ser., IV (1920), 81-86.

233. A. F. Ridley, "Special Libraries and Information Bureaux; Their Development and Future in Great Britain," *Library Association Record*, new ser., III (1925), 224-55; and Association of Special Libraries and Information Bureaux, *Reports of the Proceedings of Conferences*, vol. I (1925) to date.

234. Predeek, *Das moderne englische Bibliothekswesen*, Chapter III, with references.

235. According to Rawlings, *op. cit.*, pp. 206-8, the British Museum had forty-two large collections.

236. The statutes did not permit discard of duplicates, but the regulations were frequently broken. Finally E. M. Thompson, principal librarian from 1888 to 1909, pushed through repeal of the prohibition in the case of all dispensable duplicates (*ibid.*, p. 94).

237. Gt. Brit., Commission on the State, Discipline, Studies, and Revenues of the Uni-

versity and Colleges of Cambridge, *op. cit.*, "Evidence," pp. 16, 40 ff.; and Macray, p. 293.

238. *Ibid.*, p. 131; and Power, *op. cit.*, pp. 51-52. Cf. also Edwards, I, 553-73, for the reports of the Oxford University Commission of 1849-50.

239. Prothero, *A Memoir of Henry Bradshaw*, pp. 236 f., 310, 372 ff.

240. Esdaile, *National Libraries*, pp. 18-19; and Gt. Brit., Royal Commission on National Museums and Galleries, *Interim Report* (London, H. M. Stationery Off., 1928), p. 30 ff., and *Final Report* (London, H. M. Stationery Off., 1927), p. 13 ff.

241. The proposals of the commission of 1850 were only partially adopted. In 1877 two new commissions gave their reports, the findings of which were set forth in the Oxford and Cambridge Act. See Lord Curzon, *op. cit.*, pp. 16, 149, 162.

242. C. H. Robarts, *op. cit.*; and E. C. Thomas, *op. cit.*

243. Gt. Brit., University Grants Committee, "Quinquennial Report," *Library Association Record*, XXXVIII (1936), 191-92.

244. Esdaile, *National Libraries*, pp. 19-20; and A. R. Spofford, "Copyright in Its Relation to Libraries and Literature," *Library Journal*, I (1876), 84-89.

245. Gt. Brit., Commission on the State, Discipline, Studies, and Revenues of the University and Colleges of Cambridge, *op. cit.*, pp. 128-30. Power successfully upheld the preservation of the copyright privilege *(op. cit.*, pp. 55-56).

246. Fagan, *op. cit.*, I, 284-93; and Garnett, "The Past, the Present, and the Future of the British Museum Catalogue," *loc. cit.*, pp. 100-1. Cf. also Dziatzko, *op. cit.*

247. Oxford University, Commission Appointed by the Congregation of the University, *op. cit.*; and Margaret Burton, *Famous Libraries of the World* (London, Grafton, 1937), p. 30.

248. For income and acquisitions during the period before 1841, see Gt. Brit., Parliament, House of Commons, Select Committee on Public Libraries, *op. cit.*, "Appendix," p. 277 (Edwards); and Gt. Brit., Commissioners Appointed to Inquire into the Constitution and Government of the British Museum, *op. cit.*, "Minutes of Evidence," p. 445. For the later period see Esdaile, *National Libraries*, pp. 3-35; and Rawlings, *op. cit.*

249. Luxmoore Newcombe, *The University and College Libraries of Great Britain and Ireland; a Guide to Materials Available for the Research Student* (London, Bumpus, 1927).

250. For the history of systems of classification see Edwards, II, 761-831; E. C. Richardson, "Systems of Classification," in his *Classification, Theoretical and Practical, Together with an Appendix Containing an Essay Towards a Bibliographical History of Systems of Classification* (New York, Scribner, 1912), pp. 45-149, not included in later editions; Robert Flint, *Philosophy as a Scientia Scientarum, and a History of Classification of the Sciences* (Edinburgh, Blackwood, 1904); and W. C. Berwick Sayers, *A Manual of Classification for Librarians and Bibliographers* (London, Grafton, 1926), with an extensive bibliography on p. 321 ff.

251. Francis Bacon, *The Advancement of Human Learning* (edited by W. A. Wright, Oxford, Clarendon Press, 1869); S. T. Coleridge, *Treatise on Method, as Published in the Encyclopaedia Metropolitana* (edited by A. D. Snyder, London, Constable, 1934); and Jeremy Bentham, "Essay on Nomenclature and Classification," in his *Works* (11 vols., Edinburgh, Tait, 1843), vol. VIII.

252. Edwards, II, 779-81.

253. Reshelving of the Bodleian was done under E. W. B. Nicholson (1882-1912). See H. R. Tedder, *E. W. B. Nicholson (Bodley's Librarian, 1882-1912). In Memoriam* (Aberdeen, University Press, 1914).

254. Predeek, "Antonio Panizzi und der alphabetische Katalog des Britischen Museums," *loc. cit.*; T. H. Horne, *op. cit.*; and Edwards, II, 793-96.

255. C. T. H. Wright and C. J. Purnell, comps. *Catalogue of the London Library* (2 vols., London, 1823).

256. Power, *op. cit.*, p. 57. The classification begun by Power's predecessors had been given up as a bad job. Power presented to the commission the modern notion that the scholar is not guided by the arrangement of the books on the shelves but is led from one book to another by the footnotes and citations. He argued that the notation of the call number in the catalogue was sufficient to assure the location of a book (a point which had been urged by Dury two centuries earlier). Cf. Prothero, *A Memoir of Henry Bradshaw*, p. 372 f.

257. Dryander, *op. cit.*

258. Brown, *Manual of Library Economy* (4th ed.), and Sayers, *op. cit.*, pp. 184-96.

259. *Ibid.*, pp. 155-62.

260. *Ibid.*, pp. 135-54; and Gt. Brit., Board of Education, Public Libraries Committee, *op. cit.*, pp. 191-93.

261. Sayers, *op. cit.*, pp. 163-83.

262. *Report on Public Libraries in England and Wales*, pp. 191-93.

263. Sayers, *op. cit.*, pp. 197-209, "The Story of Classification in England."

264. Dziatzko (*op. cit.*, pp. 369-71) stated upon the occasion of his visit to the British Museum that the most outstanding deficiency was the lack of a subject catalogue. Moreover, Edwards was a confirmed supporter of the subject catalogue.

265. British Museum, *Rules for Compiling the Catalogues in the Department of Printed Books in the British Museum* (rev. ed., London, Printed by Order of the Trustees, 1927); Oxford University, Bodleian Library, *Rules for the Cataloguing of Printed Books Published Before 1920* (Oxford, University Press, 1922); Burton, *Famous Libraries*, pp. 23 f., 47 f.; Cambridge University, Library, *Rules for the Cataloguing of Printed Books, Maps, and Music* (Cambridge, University Press, 1927).

266. Greenwood, *Edward Edwards*, p. 133.

267. The *Code* of the Library Association was published in 1881 (*Library Association Monthly Notes*, I (1881), 81-84). For the Anglo-American *Code* see Rudolf Kaiser, "Die Katalogisierung," in Fritz Milkau and Georg Leyh, eds., *Handbuch der Bibliothekswissenschaft* (3 vols., Leipzig, Harrassowitz, 1931-40), II, 256-57.

268. "Report of the Commissioners Appointed to Inquire into the Constitution and Government of the British Museum, with Minutes of Evidence" (a review), *Athenaeum*, 1850, pp. 499-502; "The Universal Catalogue," *ibid.*, pp. 660-61, 716; "Universal Catalogue of Printed Books," *Journal of the Society of Arts*, XXVI (1878), 227-29; and Fritz Milkau, *Zentralkataloge und Titeldrucke; geschichtliche Erörterungen und praktische Vorschläge auf die Herstellung eines Gesamtkatalogs der preussischen wissenschaftlichen Bibliotheken* (Leipzig, Harrassowitz, 1898; *Zentralblatt für Bibliothekswesen*, "Beiheft," no. 20).

269. Cornelius Walford, "Some Practical Points in the Preparation of a General Catalogue of English Literature," *Transactions and Proceedings of the Library Association of the United Kingdom*, I (1879), 54-64, 154-55.

270. Garnett, "The British Museum Catalogue as the Basis of a Universal Catalogue," *Essays in Librarianship and Bibliography*, pp. 109-14.

271. National Central Library, *Annual Report*, XXIII (1938/1939), 46-50; and Newcombe, "Union Catalogues, National and Regional. Their Preparation and Utilisation," *Report of Proceedings of the Conference of the Association of Special Libraries and Information Bureaux*, XIII (1936), 65-75.

272. *World List of Scientific Periodicals Published in the Years 1900-1921* (2 vols., London, Oxford University Press, 1925-27; 2d ed. [covers years 1900-33], 1934); and *Union Catalogue of the Periodical Publications in the University Libraries of the British Isles* (London, Joint Standing Committee on Library Cooperation, National Central Library, 1937).

273. Gt. Brit., Board of Education, Public Libraries Committee, *op. cit.*, pp. 420-508; J. D. Cowley, "Experiments in Co-operation," *Proceedings of the Fiftieth Anniversary Conference of the Library Association*, pp. 14-22; Ernst Leipprand, "Kooper-

ationsbestrebungen im modernen englischen Bibliothekswesen," *Zentralblatt füt Bibliothekswesen*, XLVIII (1931), 601-27; and Predeek, *Das moderne englische Bibliothekswesen*, Chapter V.

274. Carnegie United Kingdom Trust, *Annual Report* (1915 to date).

275. W. G. S. Adams, *A Report on Library Provision and Policy* (Edinburgh, Carnegie United Kingdom Trustees, 1924); and J. M. Mitchell, *The Public Library System of Great Britain and Ireland* (Edinburgh, Printed for the Carnegie United Kingdom Trustees by T. and A. Constable, 1924).

276. Gt. Brit., Board of Education, Public Libraries Committee, *op. cit.*, pp. 278-366. A brief historical outline is given in Library Association, County Libraries Section, *County Libraries Manual* (edited by A. S. Cooke, London, Library Association, 1935), pp. 1-10, 167-68, "Bibliography." See also Library Association, County Libraries Section, *County Libraries in Great Britain and Ireland, Report* (1925/1926 to date).

277. Esdaile, "The Unification of the Library Resources of London," *Reports of the Proceedings of the Conference of the Association of Special Libraries and Information Bureaux*, V (1928), 65-71; and J. D. Stewart, "Possibilities in the Development of Inter-Library Relations in London and the London Area," *Library Association Record*, new ser., IV (1926), 7-21.

278. Library Association, County Libraries Section, Committee on Regional Libraries, "Regional Libraries in England," *Library Association Record*, new ser., VI (1928), 243-51.

279. L. T. Oldaker, "The Joint Standing Committee on Library Co-operation's Enquiry Office at Birmingham: a Retrospect," *Library Association Record*, 3d ser., II (1932), 118-223.

280. "Co-operation, National and International," *Year's Work in Librarianship* (1928 to date), and National Central Library, *Annual Report* (1917 to date).

281. "Opening of the Chaucer House 25th May," *Library Association Record*, 3d ser., III (1933), 169-99; and J. H. Pafford, *Library Co-operation in Europe* (London, Library Association, 1935), pp. 85-130 (union catalogues).

282. Georg Leyh, "Das Haus und seine Einrichtungen," pp. 12-15 *et passim*, in Milkau and Leyh, eds., *Handbuch der Bibliothekswissenschaft*, II, 1-115; and Predeek, *Das moderne englische Bibliothekswesen*, p. 77 ff.

283. Apparently Thomas Watts was the first to urge the construction of a reading room in the empty courtyard. In 1837 an article signed by P.P.C.R., "The New Building at the British Museum," *(loc. cit.)* appeared. It was based on a similar idea according to which the reading room was to be surrounded by galleries on four sides. In 1848 William Hosking, Professor of Architecture at King's College, published a tract, *Some Remarks upon the Recent Addition of a Reading Room to the British Museum*, in which he suggested a hall for the Antiquities Division but not a reading room. It was distinct from Panizzi's later plan. Before 1852 two further plans were suggested: Panizzi as well as the trustees had planned in 1850 another annex to the north and east sides, and in 1852 Panizzi presented his own plans which were approved by Smirke and the trustees. Hosking unjustly accused Panizzi of having used his ideas, but actually Panizzi had been inspired by the Pantheon and knew nothing of Hosking's project.

284. Gt. Brit., Commission on the State, Discipline, Studies, and Revenues of the University and Colleges in Cambridge, *op. cit.*, "Minutes of Evidence," p. 58 (Power), "Report," p. 132; H. G. Aldis, *The University Library, Cambridge* (London, Macmillan, 1922); and *idem*, "The Organisation and Methods of the Cambridge University Library," *Library Association Record*, VII (1905), 625-36.

285. James Gibbs, *Biblioteca Radcliviana* (London, Printed for the Author, 1747); and Leyh, *op. cit.*, pp. 14-15.

286. Edwards, *Lives*, p. 720 ff. (with sketches).

287. The more important studies on the Bodleian's building are: Oxford University, Commission Appointed by the Congregation of the University, *op. cit.*; H. H. E. Craster, "The Bodleian and Its Present Problems," *Library Association Record,* 3d ser., II (1932), 137-43; R. H. Hill, "Library Provision in Oxford: the Scheme in Progress," *ibid.,* 4th ser., I (1934), 103-7; and Craster, "Bodleian Library Extension," *ibid.,* XXXVIII (1936), 185-90.

288. E. Ansell, "Cambridge University Library," *Library Association Record,* 4th ser., I (1934), 399-413; and discussion by Predeek, "Die neuen englischen Bibliotheksbauten," *Zentralblatt für Bibliothekswesen,* LII (1935), 297-308.

289. Predeek, *Das moderne englische Bibliothekswesen,* pp. 97-98; and Charles Nowell, "Manchester Central Library," *Library Association Record,* 4th ser., I (1934), 243-61.

290. "The New Sheffield Central Public Library: The Building," *ibid.,* 4th ser., I (1934), 212-23; and Predeek, "Die neuen englischen Bibliotheksbauten," *loc. cit.*

291. R. Offor, "Brotherton Library of the University of Leeds," *Library Association Record,* XXXVIII (1936), 501-6.

292. Davis, *op. cit.*

293. Moses Tyson, "New Arts Library Building, Manchester," *Library Association Record,* XXXIX (1937), 425-30; "University of Liverpool; Proposed New Library," *ibid.,* XXXVIII (1936), 377-79; and Rye, "New University of London Library," *ibid.,* XXXIX (1937), 205-9.

294. Meikle, *op. cit.*

295. John Wilks, "Foster Court Science Library, University College, London," *Library Association Record,* XL (1938), 253-55.

296. Jast, *op. cit.,* p. 19.

297. Predeek, *Das moderne englische Bibliothekswesen,* pp. 83-84.

298. Conceived by E. W. B. Nicholson (London Institution, later Bodley's Librarian); held October 2-5 with the participation of 216 librarians, among them sixteen from the United States and one from Germany. The president was Winter Jones of the British Museum.

299. "Royal Charter and Bye-Laws of the Library Association," *Library Association Year Book,* 1939, pp. 65-92.

300. A splendid annalistic survey of the development of the Library Association is in the *Year Book,* 1939, pp. 29-62, "Annals of the Library Association." See also Henry Guppy, "Seventy-five Years, 1850-1925," *Library Association Record,* new ser., IV (1926), 193-213. A counterpart for Canada is the "Survey of Libraries in Canada, 1936-1938," in Canada, Bureau of Statistics, Education Branch, *Biennial Survey of Education in Canada,* 1936-38 (Ottawa, The Bureau, 1939), pt. III.

301. Library Association, *A Survey of Libraries; Reports on a Survey Made by the Library Association During 1936-1937* (London, Library Association, 1938), pp. 1-161.

302. This work was originally announced to form a chapter (or part) of the abortive *Public Library Manual,* edited by J. Y. W. Macalister and Thomas Mason, which, after the appearance of Part I (Fovargue and Ogle's *Library Legislation, 1855-1890,* in 1892), was converted into the "Library Association Series."

303. This theme had already been touched upon at the first conference of the Library Association. See Robert Harrison, "The Salaries of Librarians," *Transactions and Proceedings of the Library Association of the United Kingdom,* I (1879), 90-95.

304. Predeek, *Das moderne englische Bibliothekswesen,* p. 147 ff., with bibliography.

305. London University, School of Librarianship, *Syllabus of Information on Facilities for Training in Librarianship* (London, 1928). The revised edition was reprinted in the *Library Association Year Book,* 1939, pp. 93-111, "Syllabus of the Professional Examinations Conducted by the Library Association." The Library Association grants its own diplomas for examinations it holds. As a corporation it co-operates with the administration of the School of Librarianship. See "The New

Syllabus," *Library Association Record*, 4th ser., II (1935), 274-76; and Gt. Brit., Board of Education, Public Libraries Committee, *op. cit.*, p. 25.

306. *Ibid.*, pp. 78-92.

307. Bibliographies: F. J. Teggart, *op. cit.*; H. G. T. Cannons, *op. cit.*, continued by *Library Literature;* Burton and Vosburgh, *op. cit.* Historical accounts: In spite of extraordinarily large number of monographic studies, there are very few comprehensive works. Perhaps the most important are C. C. Jewett, *Notices of Public Libraries in the United States of America* (Washington, 1851), and W. J. Rhees, *Manual of Public Libraries, Institutions, and Societies in the United States, and British Provinces of North America* (Philadelphia, Lippincott, 1859). Neither are continuous historical accounts but only descriptions of individual libraries. Edwards, II, Chapter IV, is still valuable as a collection of material but is superseded in its details. U.S. Bureau of Education, *Public Libraries in the United States of America* (2 pts., Washington, Govt. Print. Off., 1876) is a fundamental and still indispensable official source. It is based on the works of Jewett and Rhees and on official sources after 1850. Hereafter the first part will be referred to as *Special Report*. It is introduced by an historical outline by H. E. Scudder, "Public Libraries a Hundred Years Ago," pp. 1-37. S. S. Green, *The Public Library Movement in the United States, 1853-1893* (Boston, Faxon, 1913) is based on personal reminiscences for the period after 1876. See also Melvil Dewey, "Library Progress," *The Library*, I (1889), 367-82. Brief surveys are given in the article "Libraries" in the *Encyclopaedia Britannica, loc. cit.*, and in *Cambridge History of American Literature* (4 vols., New York, Putnam, 1917-21), vols. III and IV. For public libraries in particular see Edwards, *Free Town Libraries*, III (source material and data; superseded); M. C. Tyler, "The Historic Evolution of the Free Public Library in America and Its Functions," *Library Journal*, IX (1884), 40-47; T. E. Stephens, "The Rise and Growth of the Public Library in America," *Transactions and Proceedings of the Library Association of the United Kingdom*, VI (1883), 16-30; W. J. Fletcher, *Public Libraries in America* (London, Low, 1894); R. G. Thwaites, "Ten Years of American Library Progress," *Library Journal*, XXV (1900), C 1-7; and the standard work, A. E. Bostwick, *The American Public Library* (4th ed., New York, Appleton, 1929). Official and other sources: U.S. Bureau of Education, *Report of the Commissioner of Education* (1872/1874 to date); and K. T. Moody, *Index to Library Reports* (Chicago, American Library Assn., 1913), for the reports of individual libraries, library committees, etc.

308. John Smith, *A True Relation of Such Occurrences and Accidents of Noate as Hath Hapned in Virginia* (edited by Charles Deane, Boston, Wiggins and Lunt, 1866).

309. Predeek, "Die amerikanische Bibliothek, Idee und Gestaltung," *Zentralblatt für Bibliothekswesen*, LV (1938), 468-93; "The Idea of the American Library," *Library Quarterly,* IX (1939), 445-76.

310. For example, Governor Berkeley of Virginia had the satisfaction of stating in an official report of 1671 that there were neither schools nor printing presses in the colonies. See Edward Meyer, *Die Vereinigten Staaten von Amerika* (Frankfurt, H. Keller, 1920), p. 10 f. An investigation in the beginning of the eighteenth century revealed only two parochial schools. See also T. G. Wright, *Literary Culture in Early New England, 1620-1730* (New Haven, Yale University Press, 1920).

311. Louis Shores, *Origins of the American College Library, 1638-1800* (New York, Barnes and Noble, 1934; George Peabody College for Teachers, "Contributions to Education," no. 134), and A. K. Borden, "Seventeenth-Century American Libraries," *Library Quarterly*, II (1932), 138-47.

312. Fletcher, "General Considerations Respecting Historical Research," *Special Report*, pp. 325-32.

313. Mullinger, III, 149 ff., 183 ff.

314. A. C. Potter, *The Library of Harvard University; Descriptive and Historical Notes*

(Cambridge, Harvard University Press, 1934; Harvard University, Library, "Special Publications," no. 6). The 1st and 2d eds., issued as "Bibliographical Contributions," no. 55 (1903), and no. 60 (1911), respectively, have the title *Descriptive and Historical Notes on the Library of Harvard University;* and the 3d ed. (1915) was issued as "Special Publication," no. 5. The years in which the colonial colleges were founded are: Harvard, 1636; William and Mary, 1693; Yale, 1701; Pennsylvania, 1740; Princeton, 1746; Columbia, 1754; Brown, 1764; Rutgers, 1766; and Dartmouth, 1769.

315. J. H. Tuttle, "The Libraries of the Mathers," *Proceedings of the American Antiquarian Society,* new ser., XX (1910), 269-356. The founder of the family, Richard Mather (1596-1669) came from Brasenose College, Oxford. His son, Increase Mather (1639-1723), is said to have brought the library to 136 volumes, and his son, Cotton Mather (1662-1727) to 470. The family library grew ultimately to 4,000 volumes.

316. Harvard University, Library, *Catalogus bibliotecae Harvardianae Cantabrigiae Nov-Anglorum* (Bostoniae, typis Thomae et Johannis Fleet, 1790).

317. At the outbreak of war in 1775 the Harvard Library was moved to Andover and later to Concord. In 1778 it was possible to return it without losses.

318. Among the first publications was the *Bay Psalm Book* (1640). For the history of American printing and book trade see Hellmut Lehmann-Haupt, *The Book in America* (New York, Bowker, 1939).

319. T. E. Keys, "The Colonial Library and the Development of Sectional Differences in the American Colonies," *Library Quarterly,* VIII (1938), 373-90; and Louis Booker Wright, "The Gentleman's Library in Early Virginia," *Huntington Library Quarterly,* I (1937), 3-61.

320. The statesman and great landowner William Byrd (1674-1744) owned a select library of 4,000 volumes. See R. C. Beatty, *William Byrd of Westover* (Boston, Houghton, Mifflin, 1932). The learned bibliophile and cleric Thomas Prince (1674-1744) owned an extremely valuable library in which colonial literature was well represented. James Logan of Philadelphia had a library of 3,000 volumes, and Franklin's library contained 4,276 volumes according to an inventory. See Lehmann-Haupt, *op. cit.,* pp. 253 ff., 260-61, 314-15, and P. L. Ford, *Franklin Bibliography* (Brooklyn, 1889).

321. The oldest of these collections was founded in 1653 and burned in 1747. Another one founded in 1698 was taken over by the Boston Athenaeum in 1823.

322. Thus in the Massachusetts school law of 1647, the *"magna charta* of the American public school system" (Paul Monroe, "Education," *Cambridge History of American Literature,* III, 385-424).

323. Edwards, I, 762-67; Thomas Bray, *Bibliotheca parochialis* (London, printed by E. H. for Robert Clavel, 1697); B. C. Steiner, "Rev. Thomas Bray and His American Libraries," *American Historical Review,* II (1896/1897), 59-75; and W. D. Houlette, "Parish Libraries and the Work of the Reverend Thomas Bray," *Library Quarterly,* IV (1934), 588-609.

324. Scudder, *op. cit.,* pp. 1-11; and L. P. Smith, "Public Libraries of Philadelphia," *Special Report,* pp. 953-62. The Library Company was preceded by an attempt to establish a small club library ("The Junto"). See also Lehmann-Haupt, *op. cit.,* pp. 314-15.

325. O. O. Thyregod, *Die Kulturfunktion der Bibliothek* (The Hague, Nijhoff, 1936), p. 67.

326. L. P. Smith, *op. cit.,* p. 954.

327. Lehmann-Haupt, *op. cit.,* p. 315. There was also the Deutsche Gesellschaft in Pennsylvanien, which was founded to protect the legal rights and to relieve the distress of German immigrants in Pennsylvania. In 1766 it was decided to found a library (not realized until 1783) to ameliorate the "ägyptische Finsternis in Deutsch-Pennsylvanien." See Oswald Seidensticker, *Geschichte der deutschen Gesellschaft*

von Pennsylvanien, (Philadelphia, Kohler, 1876), pp. 201-7; and A. B. Faust, "Übersicht über die Geschichte der Deutschen in Amerika," p. 63, in Max Heinrici, ed., *Das Buch der Deutschen in Amerika* (Philadelphia, Walther's Buchdruckerei, 1909), pp. 49-82.

328. The leading publication of this period was *The Federalist*, in which the brilliant articles of Madison, Hamilton, and Jay appeared. See also the informative book of B. J. Hendrick, *The Bulwark of the Republic* (Boston, Little, Brown, 1937).

329. This stipulation affects authors' rights.

330. *Special Report*, pp. xii-xiii.

331. Boston Athenaeum, *The Athenaeum Centenary; the Influence and History of the Boston Athenaeum from 1807 to 1907* (Boston, Boston Athenaeum, 1907).

332. After 1830 railroads ran into the interior of the continent, and by 1838 the first highway reached the Mississippi. As early as 1816 the first American paper machine had been patented, and a type-casting and type-setting machine followed in 1822. Printing began in 1834 in Santa Fé with a *Cuaderno de ortografía* and in 1846 in San Francisco. About the same time more than 400 paper mills were in operation. See Lehmann-Haupt, *op. cit.*, p. 118 ff.

333. C. B. Joeckel, *The Government of the American Public Library* (Chicago, University of Chicago Press, 1935); F. B. Perkins, "Young Men's Mercantile Libraries," *Special Report*, pp. 383, 385; G. L. Smith, "Public Libraries of Baltimore," *ibid.*, pp.844-46; W. H. Venable, "Public Libraries of Cincinnati," *ibid.*, pp. 901-2; L. P. Smith, *op. cit.*, pp. 973-74; and A. E. Whitaker, "Public Libraries of San Francisco and of the Pacific Coast," *Special Report*, pp. 1004-5.

334. There are several pertinent articles in the *Special Report* which deal with apprentices' and mercantile libraries.

335. Erich Hylla, "Bildungswesen der Vereinigten Staaten," p. 245 ff., in *Handbuch der Amerikakunde* (Frankfurt, Diesterweg, 1931), with a bibliography of the most important literature. The first regulations on school books were passed by Massachusetts, New York, and Michigan in 1837 and by Rhode Island in 1840.

336. "School and Asylum Libraries," *Special Report*, pp. 38-59; and Joeckel, *op. cit.*, p. 112 ff. *et passim*.

337. W. F. Yust, *Library Legislation* (2d ed., Chicago, American Library Assn., 1921; "Manual of Library Economy," Chapter IX), and M. F. Ferguson, comp., *American Library Laws* (Chicago, American Library Assn., 1930).

338. The method of handing over property, administrative, and supervisory rights of a foundation or municipal institution to a board, as is the general custom with local governments in accordance with old English law, has become the role not only for public libraries but also for many endowed and research libraries. The boards have usually proven themselves to be reliable and nonpartisan intermediaries between libraries, citizenry, and municipal administrations. See Joeckel, *op. cit.*, *passim;* and Predeek, "Rechtsstellung und Verwaltung der amerikanischen Public Library," in *Otto Glauning zum 60. Geburtstag* (2 vols., Leipzig, Richard Hadl, 1936), I, 163-73.

339. F. B. Perkins, "Public Libraries of Boston and Vicinity," *Special Report*, pp. 863-72 (Boston Public Library); Edwards, II, 214-16; W. F. Poole, "The Public Library of Our Time," *Library Journal*, XII (1887), 311-20; and H. G. Wadlin, *The Public Library of the City of Boston* (Boston, Boston Public Library, 1911).

340. Jewett (1816-68) worked in the Brown University Library from 1841 to 1847, was director of the Smithsonian Library from 1847 to 1855, and superintendent of the Boston Public Library from 1857 to 1868. See R. A. Guild, "Memorial Sketch of Professor C. Jewett," *Library Journal*, XII (1887), 507-11; and Cyrus Adler, "The Smithsonian Library," in E. B. Goode, ed., *The Smithsonian Institution, 1846-1896; the History of Its First Half Century* (Washington, 1897), pp. 264-302.

341. Justin Winsor (1831-97) was director of the Boston Public Library from 1868 to

1877, and of the Harvard University Library from 1877 to 1897. See W. C. Lane, "Justin Winsor, Librarian and Historian—1831-1897," *Library Journal*, XXIII (1898), 7-13. Winsor's reports are of greatest importance because of their generalized character. See the bibliography of his writings in Harvard University, Library, "Bibliographical Contributions," no. 54 (1902).

342. George Ticknor (1791-1871), *Life, Letters and Journals* (2 vols., edited by G. S. Hillard, Boston, Houghton, Mifflin, 1876). See also J. D. M. Ford, "George Ticknor," *Dictionary of American Biography*, XVIII, 525-28.

343. Ticknor, *op. cit.*, II, 300 ff.

344. H. G. Pearson, "Edward Everett," *Dictionary of American Biography*, VI, 223-26.

345. The organizer and director was Joseph Green Cogswell (1786-1871), who had studied with Ticknor in Göttingen and travelled in Europe with Everett.

346. Edwards, II, 216-18. The first public library established under this statute was in New Bedford.

347. Among these were 628 school libraries, 182 college libraries, 128 society libraries, and 467 special libraries. See "Library Reports and Statistics," *Special Report*, pp. 745-836. The *Special Report* notes a total of 3,682 libraries in 1875 (p. xvi).

348. H. A. Homes, "State and Territorial Libraries," *Special Report*, pp. 292-311.

349. Only the New York State Library in Albany had as many as 95,000 volumes in 1875.

350. E. C. Richardson, "The National Library Problem To-day," *Library Journal*, XXX (1905), C 3-9, gives a recapitulation of developments in this field; H. M. Utley, "Government, Constitution, By-Laws, and Trustees," *Library Journal*, XVIII (1893), 225-27; A. R. Spofford, "Aids to Library Progress by the Government of the United States," *Library Journal*, XVIII, 189-249; and Herbert Putnam, "Relation of State Libraries to the Library of Congress," *Library Journal*, XXV (1900), 729-33.

351. Smithsonian Institution, *Annual Report*, I (1848), p. 36.

352. The principal work is W. D. Johnston, *History of the Library of Congress*, vol. 1, 1800-64 (Washington, Govt. Print. Off., 1904, "Contributions to American Library History;" no. 1). In addition see U.S. Library of Congress, *Report of the Librarian of Congress* (1897 to date; 1901, pp. 183-97, contains an historical outline); Herbert Putnam, "The Library of Congress as a National Library," *Library Journal*, XXX (1905), C 27-34; and W. W. Bishop, *The Library of Congress* (Washington, American Library Assn., 1911).

353. Such important men as Edward Everett, the educator Horace Mann, the philologist George Marsh, the mathematician James Mills Peirce, and the eloquent Senator Rufus Choate were on the library committee in those days.

354. W. C. Winlock, "The International Exchange System," in E. B. Goode, *op. cit.*, pp. 397-418; and Adler, *op. cit.*

355. Jewett, *On the Construction of Catalogues of Libraries and Their Publication by Means of Separate Stereotyped Titles, With Rules and Examples* (2d ed., Washington, Smithsonian Institution, 1853).

356. Friedrich von Raumer, *Die Vereinigten Staaten von Nordamerika* (2 vols., Leipzig, Brockhaus, 1845), II, 90, 112 ff., 238.

357. Fletcher, "Public Libraries in Manufacturing Communities," *Special Report*, pp. 403-11. In 1823 in Philadelphia the library of the Franklin Institute for the Promotion of Manufactures and the Mechanic and Useful Arts was founded. It was followed in 1824 by the Rensselaer Polytechnic Institute and in 1845 by the Engineering College in Schenectady. See Spratt, *op. cit.*, p. 128 ff.; and Thyregod, *op. cit.*, pp. 157 f., 166 f.

358. "Libraries of the Central Government," *Special Report*, pp. 252-78; "College Libraries," *ibid.*, pp. 60-126; S. B. Griswold, "Law Libraries," *ibid.*, pp. 161-70; and J. S. Billings, "Medical Libraries in the United States," *ibid.*, pp. 171-82.

359. See the splendid work of J. A. Walz, *German Influence in American Education and Culture* (Philadelphia, Carl Schurz Memorial Foundation, 1936).

360. H. P. Tappan, *University Education* (New York, Putnam, 1851).
361. B. A. Hinsdale, *History of the University of Michigan* (Ann Arbor, Published by the University, 1906); C. H. Haskins, "The Graduate School of Arts and Sciences, 1872-1929," in S. E. Morison, ed., *The Development of Harvard University, 1869-1929* (Cambridge, Harvard University Press, 1930), pp. 451-52; Charles W. Eliot, *Harvard Memories* (Cambridge, Harvard University Press, 1923); D. C. Gilman, *The Launching of a University* (New York, Dodd, Mead, 1906); and Abraham Flexner, *Universities, American, English, and German* (New York, Oxford University Press, 1930).
362. Potter, *op. cit.*, pp. 20, 121; and Paul Trommsdorf, [Review of Potter's *The Library of Harvard University*], *Zentralblatt für Bibliothekswesen*, XXI (1904), 253-54.
363. Seymour de Ricci, *English Collectors of Books and Manuscripts (1530-1930)* (Cambridge, Harvard University Press, 1930), p. 121; and idem, *Census of Medieval and Renaissance Manuscripts in the United States and Canada* (3 vols., New York, Wilson, 1935-40), I, 1637 ff. Some manuscripts were acquired by the Union Theological Seminary in New York, but the greater part was purchased by Sir Thomas Phillips of Cheltenham.
364. Lücke's books went to the Harvard Divinity School, and those of Niedner went to the Andover Theological Seminary at Harvard (Potter, *op. cit.*, p. 144 f.). The Chicago Theological Seminary acquired Hengstenberg's library. See T. W. Goodspeed, *A History of the University of Chicago* (Chicago, University of Chicago Press, 1916), p. 26.
365. Bopp's and Zarncke's libraries went to Cornell, Bernays' to Toronto, Scherer's to Adelbert College in Cleveland, and Pott's and Bechstein's to Pennsylvania. See Georg Witkowski, "Deutsche Bibliotheken auf der Auswanderung nach Amerika" (abstract of article in *Nationalzeitung*, no. 228, April 10, 1902, morning edition), *Zentralblatt für Bibliothekswesen*, XIX (1902), 255.
366. Anna de Lagarde, *Paul de Lagarde, Erinnerungen aus seinem Leben* (Göttingen, Dieterich's Verlag, 1894), p. 150; K. L. Schemann, *Paul de Lagarde* (2d ed.; Leipzig, E. Matthes, 1920), p. 88; and Richard Pietschmann, "Wissenschaftliche Arbeitsbibliotheken," *Preussische Jahrbücher*, CXXII (1905), 71-72. Heinzel's library went to George Washington.
367. Sauppe's library went to Bryn Mawr, Brunn's to Vassar, Hertz's to Virginia, Ribbeck's to McGill (Witkowski, *op. cit.*), and Wachsmuth's to George Washington.
368. Curtius' 7,000 volumes went to Yale (*ibid.*). For Ranke's see *ibid.*; for Maurer's, see Potter, *op. cit.*, pp. 90, 125.
369. Georg Fischer, "Wilhelm Baum," *Allgemeine deutsche Biographie*, XLVI (Nachträge), 250-54. For Du Bois-Reymond see Pietschmann, *op. cit.*, p. 76. The scientific and medical portions of both libraries went to the John Crerar Library in 1906 *(Annual Report*, XII [1907], 14).
370. Potter, *op. cit.*, pp. 120-22.
371. *Ibid.*, p. 89 f.; and Pietschmann, *op. cit.*
372. For example, see Witkowski, *op. cit.*; Camillo von Klenze, "Auswanderung deutscher Gelehrtenbibliotheken nach Amerika" (abstract of article in *Allgemeine Zeitung, Beilage*, July 27, 1905), *Zentralblatt für Bibliothekswesen*, XXII (1905), 549; and Fritz Milkau, "Die Abteilung für niederdeutsche Literatur bei der Universitätsbibliothek zu Greifswald," *ibid.*, XXIV (1907), 64.
373. Pietschmann, *op. cit.*
374. W. W. Bishop, "Some Newer Responsibilities of American Librarians," *Zentralblatt für Bibliothekswesen*, L (1933), 106-11.
375. U.S.Bureau of Education, "College Libraries," *loc. cit.*, gives only general remarks and individual sketches; "Library Reports and Statistics," *ibid.*, 745-836; Fletcher, "Yearly Report on College Libraries," *Library Journal*, X (1885), 267-69, gives the results of a questionnaire on holdings, income, lending policy, and other matters

in some fifteen colleges; L. Ambrose, "College Libraries," *Library Journal,* XVIII (1893), 113-19; W. N. C. Carlton, "College Libraries in the Mid-Nineteenth Century," *Library Journal,* XXXII (1907), 479-86; D. B. Gilchrist, "The Evolution of College and University Libraries," *Bulletin of the American Library Association,* XX (1926), 293-99; and Bishop, "Our College and University Libraries—a Survey and a Program," in his *Backs of Books* (Baltimore, Williams and Wilkins, 1926), pp. 202-25 (originally published in *School and Society,* XII [1920], 205-14).

376. The *Special Report* of 1876 shows altogether 312 college libraries with almost 2,000,000 volumes. In 1885 only 4 out of 456 libraries had more than 100,000 volumes, 13 more than 50,000, and 40 more than 25,000.

377. Student collections also arose with the colleges in most cases. Many of them have existed until the present day or have passed over into the general libraries, as, for example, the Linonian and Brothers Libraries (each with 13,000 volumes) founded at Yale in 1769.

378. In the winter of 1877 Trinity College Library in Hartford, was open once a week, lent 680 volumes from a total of 15,000. The University of Minnesota library, about the same size and open daily, lent 3,000 volumes and counted 225 readers daily.

379. J. H. Canfield, "The Library," p. 427 ff., in Columbia University, *A History of Columbia University, 1754-1904* (New York, Lemke and Büchner, 1904).

380. J. C. M. Hanson, "Some Observations on the Departmental Library Problem in Universities, with Special Reference to the University of Chicago Libraries," *Bulletin of the American Library Association,* VI (1912), 280-92.

381. Goodspeed, *op. cit.,* pp. 134-36; and A. T. Dorf, "The University of Chicago Libraries," *Library Quarterly,* IV (1934), 185-97.

382. Bishop, "Our College and University Libraries—a Survey and a Program," *loc. cit.,* pp. 202-5.

383. Under a grant from the Carnegie Corporation, Bishop and others conducted in 1929 a statistical investigation of two hundred college libraries. It was revealed that most of them contained only a small proportion of the 14,000 titles from a standard list drawn up by themselves. For the results see W. M. Randall, *The College Library* (Chicago, American Library Assn., 1932), pp. 85 ff., 162.

384. Ticknor, for whom the University of Göttingen was a model, saw in the Cambridge Museum and the Harvard Law School the finest institutions in the country and the beginning of a true university *(op. cit.,* II, 422).

385. Theodore Gill, "Scientific Libraries in the United States," *Special Report,* pp. 183-217.

386. Green, "The Library and Its Relation to Persons Engaged in Industrial Pursuits," *Library Journal,* XIV (1889), 215-25; G. R. Humphrey, "Librarians and the Working Classes," *Library Association Monthly Notes,* IV (1883), 58-61; and C. C. Soule, "The Library and the Industrial Classes," *Library Journal,* XVII (1892), 90-92.

387. J. C. Dana, *Libraries: Addresses and Essays* (New York, Wilson, 1916).

388. Special Libraries Association, *Special Libraries Directory of the United States and Canada* (New York, 1921; 2d ed., 1925; 3d ed., 1935). See also Lehmann-Haupt, *op. cit.,* p. 361.

389. Chairs have been established for music (1925), American history (1927), fine arts (1927), aeronautics (1929), and geography (1929). See *Report of the Librarian of Congress,* 1924/1925, pp. 3-7, "Elizabeth Sprague Coolidge Gift."

390. Lehmann-Haupt, *op. cit.,* p. 299.

391. *The Huntington Library Bulletin,* nos. 1-11, 1931 to 1937, continued by *The Huntington Library Quarterly,* vol. I, 1937 to date; Henry E. Huntington Library, *Annual Report,* no. 1, 1927/1928 to date; Henry E. Huntington Library, *Huntington Library Publications* (San Marino, Calif., 1937); Pierpont Morgan Library, *The Pierpont Morgan Library . . . 1924-1929* (New York, Plandome Press [priv.], 1930) and subsequent quinquennial reports; Folger Shakespeare Library, *The Folger*

Notes

Shakespeare Library, Washington (Washington, 1933); Bogeng, *op. cit.*, I, 466-77; and Lehmann-Haupt, *op. cit.*, pp. 299 ff., 360.

392. U.S.Bureau of Education, "Statistics of Public, Society, and School Libraries Having 5,000 Volumes and over in 1908," *Bulletin*, 1909, no. 5.

393. See Borden, "The Sociological Beginnings of the Library Movement," *Library Quarterly*, I (1931), 278-82.

394. The rate for libraries according to the tax laws was levied in mills (thousandths of a dollar) on assessed real property. In some states the rate was one-half mill, in others three-fourths mill, and in a few more than one mill. By World War I the library's portion of municipal appropriations had been raised from an average of ten cents to sixty cents per person, but for the schools it increased from forty to fifty dollars per person. Accordingly, the library's quota of total municipal expenditures remained at about 1.3 per cent, while the schools received forty to fifty dollars to every one for libraries.

395. T. W. Koch, *A Book of Carnegie Libraries* (New York, Wilson, 1917), and B. J. Hendrick, *The Life of Andrew Carnegie* (2 vols., New York, Doubleday, Doran, 1932). A total of $65,000,000 is estimated as the sum spent for the Carnegie libraries.

396. H. M. Lydenberg, *History of the New York Public Library: Astor, Lenox and Tilden Foundations* (New York, New York Public Library, 1923), p. 407 f.

397. Carnegie Corporation of New York, *Report of Informal Conferences on Library Interests* (New York, 1931).

398. For the special literature see the bibliographies of Cannons, Vosburgh, and Lehmann-Haupt.

399. C. F. D. Belden, "The Library Service of Herbert Putnam in Boston," in *Essays Offered to Herbert Putnam* (New Haven, Yale University Press, 1929), pp. 10-14. The first branch library had been opened in 1870.

400. Lydenberg, *op. cit.*; and Henry Stevens, *Recollections of Mr. James Lenox of New York, and the Formation of His Library* (London, Stevens, 1887).

401. For example, New York had more than fifty branches in 1924, Brooklyn had thirty-four, Chicago forty-three, Los Angeles forty-one, Knoxville two.

402. S. S. Green, "The Relation of the Public Library to the Public School," *Library Journal*, V (1880), 235-45; *idem*, "Report on Libraries and the Schools," *ibid.*, VIII (1883), *idem*, "Work with Library and School in Worcester," *ibid.*, XII (1887), 119-21; *idem*, "Libraries and Schools," *ibid.*, XVI (1891), C 22-26; Green *et al.*, "Work Between Libraries and Schools: a Symposium," *ibid.*, XXII (1897), 181-87; and Borden, "The Sociological Beginnings of the Library Movement," *loc. cit.*

403. Joeckel, *op. cit.*, pp. 263-303.

404. H. C. Long, *County Library Service* (Chicago, American Library Assn., 1925), with an exhaustive bibliography; and for the South the basic works of L. R. Wilson and E. A. Wight, *County Library Service in the South* (Chicago, University of Chicago Press, 1935).

405. Joeckel, *op. cit.*, pp. 304-40; *idem*, "Library Service," U.S. Advisory Committee on Education, *Staff Study*, no. 11 (1938), for a brilliant and exhaustive treatment of the subject. See also H. W. Odum, *Southern Regions in the United States* (Chapel Hill, University of North Carolina Press, 1936).

406. Bishop, "Resources of American Libraries," *Library Quarterly*, VIII (1938), 445-79.

407. On this point see Wilhelm Munthe, *American Librarianship from a European Angle* (Chicago, American Library Assn., 1939) particularly Chapter II, "Books and Reading in America and Europe," and Chapter VII, "A Pessimist Looks at the Public Library."

408. Goodspeed, *op. cit.*, p. 134 *et passim*. For adult education and university library extension the following are particularly important: American Library Association, Committee on Library Extension, *Library Extension; a Study of Public Library Conditions and Needs* (Chicago, American Library Assn., 1926) with many refer-

ences; American Library Association, *Libraries and Adult Education* (New York, American Library Assn., 1926); W. H. Lighty, "The Essential Partnership of University Extension Teaching and the Library in the Field of Adult Education," *Bulletin of the American Library Association*, XX (1926), 559-61; C. H. Milam, "Libraries and Adult Education," in American Association for Adult Education, *Handbook of Adult Education in the United States*, 1934, pp. 70-97.

409. On the war work of the American Library Association see G. B. Utley, "The Library of War Service and Its General Director," in *Essays Offered to Herbert Putnam*, pp. 474-91.

410. Munthe, *op. cit.*, p. 69.

411. Douglas Waples, *People and Print; Social Aspects of Reading in the Depression* (Chicago, University of Chicago Press, 1937); also published in *Bulletin of the Social Science Research Council*, no. 37 (1937), with the title, "Research Memorandum on Social Aspects of Reading in the Depression."

412. Bishop, "Resources of American Libraries," *loc. cit.*

413. L. R. Wilson, *The Geography of Reading* (Chicago, University of Chicago Press, 1938), pp. 445-60, with a selected but extensive bibliography.

414. See also Munthe, *op. cit.*, p. 43 ff.

415. The richest library of incunabula is the Huntington Library with more than 5,100 imprints. For manuscript holdings see de Ricci, *Census of Medieval Manuscripts*. The Henry Walters collection in Baltimore contains more than 300 incunabula. It is described by Walters in his *Incunabula Typographica; a Descriptive Catalogue of the Books Printed in the Fifteenth Century (1460-1500) in the Library of Henry Walters* (Baltimore, 1906). In 1919 the Bibliographical Society of America, *Census of Fifteenth Century Books Owned in America* (New York, New York Public Library, 1919), revealed 169 public and 246 private libraries with 13,200 volumes and 6,640 titles; Fremont Rider, "Holdings of Incunabula in American University Libraries," *Library Quarterly*, IX (1939), 273-84, lists 20,813; M. B. Stilwell, *Incunabula and Americana, 1450-1800* (New York, Columbia University Press, 1931).

416. Thorvald Solberg, "The United States and International Copyright," in *Essays Offered to Herbert Putnam*, pp. 410-22. Solberg also wrote an historical outline in the *Report of the Librarian of Congress* for 1902/1903 (Report of the Register of Copyrights on Copyright Legislation," pp. 437-589).

417. *Report of the Librarian of Congress* (Herbert Putnam), 1898 to 1939; *ibid.*, 1901/1902, is a basic report on conditions and holdings; and W. A. Slade, "Some Notes on the Library of Congress as a Center of Research," *ibid.*, 1937/1938, pp. 450-66, with a statistical table showing growth of holdings from 1898 to 1938.

418. P. 102 ff. See also C. B. Shaw, comp., *A List of Books for College Libraries* (2d ed., Chicago, American Library Assn., 1931).

419. Justin Winsor, "Library Memoranda," *Special Report*, pp. 711-14.

420. Bishop, "Resources of American Libraries," *loc. cit.*, p. 478. On the whole the university libraries were able to triple their holdings between 1914 and 1935.

421. See Joeckel, "Library Service," *loc. cit.*; and Munthe, *op. cit.*, p. 126 f.

422. Spratt, *op. cit.*, p. 132 ff. For the rich holdings of the special libraries see the *Special Libraries Directory*, and J. H. Canfield, "The Specialization of Libraries," *Library Journal*, XXVIII (1903), 820-22.

423. Wilson, *Geography of Reading*, pp. 191-93. Total holdings may be reckoned thus: 1,460 college and university libraries, 53,000,000 volumes; 1,475 special libraries, 27,000,000 volumes; 6,235 public libraries, 100,000,000 volumes; 166 federal libraries in Washington, 11,000,000 volumes; 135 state libraries, 12,000,000 volumes; and if the school libraries are listed in addition, then the total is increased by 27,000,000 volumes more.

424. Cutter, "Library Catalogues," *Special Report*, pp. 526-622, with a chronological list of all catalogues printed since 1723. The first catalogue was printed by Harvard

University Library, *Catalogus librorum Bibliotecae collegij Harvardini* (Bostoni Nov. Anglorum, typis B. Green, Academiae typographi, 1723). Thirty-eight catalogues had appeared in print by 1800 (Potter, *op. cit.*, p. 60).

425. Johnston, *op. cit.*, p. 147 ff., and Appendix V.

426. Potter and C. K. Bolton, *The Librarians of Harvard College* (Cambridge, Harvard University Library, 1897; "Bibliographical Contributions," no. 52); Potter, *op. cit.*, p. 24 f.

427. Milkau, *Centralkataloge und Titeldrucke*, p. 27 ff.; and H. C. Bolton, "Bibliography," in E. B. Goode, ed., *op. cit.*, pp. 785-804.

428. Above all there was the *Index Catalogue of the Surgeon General's Library* begun in 1874. When Billings became director of the New York Public Library in 1896, he began a new *Index Catalogue* in 1897 with similar objectives and designed as a kind of supplement to Poole's *Index of Periodicals*. The Library of Congress, John Crerar, and the Boston Public Library cooperated, and by 1911 it had grown to over 1,250,000 cards. See Lydenberg, *John Shaw Billings* (Chicago, American Library Assn., 1924; Bostwick, ed., "Library Pioneers," no. 1) and J. S. Billings, "Medical Libraries in the United States," *Special Report*, pp. 171-82.

429. Cutter, "Rules for a Printed Dictionary Catalogue," *ibid.*, part II.

430. Charles Martel, "Cataloguing: 1876-1926," *Bulletin of the American Library Association*, XX (1926), 492-98; also appeared in American Library Association, Catalog Section, *Catalogers' and Classifiers' Yearbook*, I (1929), 93-103, and *Library Journal*, LI (1926), 1065-69; American Library Association, Catalog Rules Committee, "Report," *Bulletin of the American Library Association*, I (1907), 47-52, II (1908), 171-73, and III (1909), 224-25; American Library Association, *Catalog Rules: Author and Title Entries* (American ed., Chicago, The Association, 1908); Kaiser, "Vergleichung der englisch-amerikanischen Katalogregeln mit der preussischen Instruktion und die Frage einer internationalen Einigung," *Zentralblatt für Bibliothekswesen*, XXVIII (1911), 412-30; Pierce Butler, "James Christian Meinich Hanson," *Library Quarterly*, IV (1934), 127-35; Hanson, *Comparative Study of Cataloguing Rules Based on the Anglo-American Code of 1908, with Comments on the Rules and on the Prospects for a Further Extension of International Agreement and Cooperation* (Chicago, University of Chicago Press, 1939).

431. Hanson, "The Library of Congress and Its New Catalogue; Some Unwritten History," in *Essays Offered to Herbert Putnam*, pp. 178-94; and W. C. Ford, "An Old-Fashioned Librarian, the Late A. R. Spofford," *Library Journal*, XXXIII (1908), 356-58.

432. C. H. Hastings, "Reminiscences and Observations," in *Essays Offered to Herbert Putnam*, pp. 195-206.

433. American Library Association, Committee on Resources of American Libraries, *Report of the Informal Conference on Union Catalogues* (Chicago, American Library Assn., 1936); Bishop, "Union Catalogs," *Library Quarterly*, VII (1937), 36-49, and "Resources of American Libraries," *loc. cit.*

434. Union catalogues limited to regional coverage have been started in Denver, Philadelphia, Cleveland, and elsewhere. See Joeckel, "Library Service," *loc. cit.*, pp. 57, 72 f., M. F. Tauber, "Other Aspects of Union Catalogs," *Library Quarterly*, IX (1939), 411-31.

435. Martel, "The Library of Congress Classification; Some Considerations Regarding the Relation of Book or Library Classification to the 'Order of the Sciences'," in *Essays Offered to Herbert Putnam*, pp. 327-32; Bishop, "J. C. M. Hanson and International Cataloging," *Library Quarterly*, IV (1934), 166.

436. For a complete history of American library buildings see the account of Leyh, *op. cit.*, in which the author has discussed the development in its entirety for the first time. Pertinent literature is included, particularly on p. 39.

437. Potter and C. K. Bolton, *op. cit.*, pp. 27, 39 f. See also *Annual Report of the Har-*

vard University Library during the administration of Justin Winsor. Space shortage is given special attention in reports after 1889.

438. F. W. Ashley, "Three Eras in the Library of Congress," in *Essays Offered to Herbert Putnam*, pp. 57-67; and C. R. Barnett, "Size Factor in Library Problems,"
ibid., pp. 68-79.

439. Winsor, "Library Buildings," *Special Report*, pp. 465-75.

440. Munthe, *Amerikanske biblioteker* (Uppsala, Almqvist och Wiksell, 1931); also appeared in *Nordisk tidskrift för bok- och biblioteksväsen*, XVIII (1931), 85-119;
resumé by Hanson, "Wilhelm Munthe on 'American Libraries'," *Library Quarterly*,
II (1932), 151-56. The same material was covered by Munthe in "Die neuesten amerikanischen Bibliotheken," *Zentralblatt für Bibliothekswesen*, XLVIII (1931), 447-78,
of which there was an English translation, "Modern American Library Buildings,"
Library Association Record, 3d ser., II (1932), 238-44, 283-90, 341-46, 371-79;
Munthe, *American Librarianship from a European Angle*, pp. 174-84. For the specialized literature see the bibliographies of Burton and Vosburgh (pp. 116-18) and
Cannons.

441. Munthe, *American Librarianship from a European Angle*, p. 101 f.

442. *Report of the Librarian of Congress*, 1937/1938, pp. 1-3 (on the Annex; picture and
plans between pp. 32 and 33).

443. The librarian of the colonial period was not a professional librarian but rather a
"scholar," a member of the college, who was entrusted for a period of varying
length with the administration of the library. See Shores, *op. cit.*; Potter and
Bolton, *op. cit.*

444. L. P. Smith, "Qualifications for a Librarian," *Library Journal*, I (1876), 69-74.

445. Hanson, "The Library of Congress and Its New Catalogue; Some Unwritten History," p. 179, *loc. cit.*

446. Poole, "The Organization and Management of Public Libraries," *Special Report*,
p. 489.

447. Melvil Dewey, "School of Library Economy," *Library Journal*, VIII (1883), 285-91;
and Cutter, "School of Library Economy," *Library Journal*, VIII, (1883), 293-95. For
the documentary history of the founding of Dewey's school, see Columbia University, School of Library Service, *School of Library Economy at Columbia College,
1887-1889* (New York, Columbia University, School of Library Service, 1937). See
also Bostwick, *op. cit.*, Chapter XXVII.

448. American Library Association, Board of Education for Librarianship, "Annual
Report, 1925/1926," *Bulletin of the American Library Association*, XX (1926),
405-73; E. J. Reece, *The Curriculum in Library Schools* (New York, Columbia University Press, 1936).

449. Columbia University, School of Library Service, *op. cit.*, p. 40.

450. Flexner, *op. cit.*, p. 123, note 1.

451. C. C. Williamson, *Training for Library Service* (New York, Carnegie Corporation
of New York, 1923), and Ralph Munn, *Condition and Trends in Education for
Librarianship* (New York, Carnegie Corporation of New York, 1936).

452. F. P. Keppel, "The Carnegie Corporation and the Graduate Library School: a
Historical Outline," *Library Quarterly*, I (1931), 22-25; and Waples, "The Graduate
Library School at Chicago," *ibid.*, 26-36.

453. Butler, *An Introduction to Library Science* (Chicago, University of Chicago Press,
1933); Leon Carnovsky, "Why Graduate Study in Librarianship?" *Library Quarterly*,
VII (1937), 246-61; J. P. Danton, "A Plea for a Philosophy of Librarianship," *ibid.*,
IV (1934), 16-27; and, in a skeptical mood, H. E. Bliss, "As to a Philosophy of Librarianship," *ibid.*, 232-35.

454. "American Library Institute," *Bulletin of the American Library Association*, I
(1907), Handbook, p. 21, and II (1908), Handbook, p. 62. This group was the fore-

runner of the new Library Institute. See L. R. Wilson, ed., *Library Trends* (Chicago, University of Chicago Press, 1937), "Introduction."

455. Bostwick, ed., *Popular Libraries of the World* (Chicago, American Library Assn., 1933), p. 285 f.

456. Between September 15 and September 17, 1853 the world's first library convention, called together by Jewett, met. Eighty-two librarians and bookdealers participated. Political tension of the period during the War Between the States nullified hopes put forward at the time. See *Special Report*, pp. xxvii; Fletcher, "William Frederick Poole," *Library Journal*, XIX (1894), 81-83; W. E. Foster, "Five Men of '76," *Bulletin of the American Library Association*, XX (1926), 312-23.

457. Of the extensive literature on the history of the American Library Association the following are particularly valuable: *Proceedings of the Librarians' Convention Held in New York City, September 15, 16, and 17, 1853* (Cedar Rapids, Iowa, 1915); Dewey, "Past, Present, and Future of the A.L.A.," *Library Journal*, V (1880), 247-76; Poole, "Address of the President" (history of the American Library Association), *ibid.*, XI (1886), 199-204; Green, *Public Library Movement in the United States;* G. B. Utley, *Fifty Years of the American Library Association* (Chicago, American Library Assn., 1929); R. R. Bowker, "Seed Time and Harvest—the Story of the A.L.A.," *Bulletin of the American Library Association*, XX (1926), 303-9; Bostwick, *The American Public Library,* Chapter XXVII; and G. G. Dawe, *Melvil Dewey, Seer; Inspirer; Doer, 1851-1931* (Lake Placid, 1932).

458. American Library Association, Third Activities Committee (Charles H. Brown, chairman), "Tentative Report," *Bulletin of the American Library Association*, XXXIII (1939), 361-448, and "Final Report," *ibid.*, 782-804. The first is also a comprehensive report on the development and policies of the organization.

459. Nevertheless, there have been local efforts in the direction of trade unions, and at present there are six of them. See B. R. Berelson, "Library Unionization," *Library Quarterly*, IX (1939), 477-510.

460. "A National Plan for Libraries," *Bulletin of the American Library Association*, XXIX (1935), 91-98, and XXXIII (1939), 137-50.

INDEX

Accession records, 26, 46, 139
Acquisition policies, 4, 8, 13, 18, 22, 25-6, 31, 32, 35-8, 42, 44, 47, 63, 64-7, 101-2, 103, 106, 114-17, 125
Acton, Lord, 46
Acts of Dissolution, 5
Acts of Supremacy, 8
Acts of Uniformity, 8
Adams, Charles K., 99
Adams, John, 95
Adams, W. G. S., 70-1, 72, 147
Adamson, J. J., 136, 137
Addison, Joseph, 25, 137
Adelbert College Library, 153
Adjustable classification, 68
Adler, Cyrus, 151, 152
Administration. *See* Library administration
Adult education, 58, 112, 113, 155, 156
Adult Education Committee (England), 56, 144
Advocates' Library, 26, 27, 49-50, 137
   building, 74, 141
   catalogue, 26
Aeronautical literature, 154
Alchemical literature, 16
Aldis, H. G., 136, 147
Alexandrian Library, 96
Alfred the Great, 5
All Souls College Library, Oxford, 26, 44
Althorp Library, 51, 141
Alvarez Espriella, Manuel, 136-7
Ambrose, L., 154
American Association of Law Libraries, 128
American Indian collections, 106
American Library Association, 98, 105, 107, 108, 112, 118, 119, 125, 127-9, 159
   Board of Education for Librarianship, 125, 158
   Catalog Rules Committee, 157
   Catalog Section, 157

College and Reference Section, 128
Committee on Library Extension, 155
Committee on Resources of American Libraries, 157
Council, 128
Executive Board, 128
Philadelphia Conference, 1876, 76, 126
publications, 129
Third Activities Committee, 159
Trustees' Section, 128
American Library Institute, 158
American Revolution, 85, 86, 88, 115
Americana, 36, 115, 116
"Americanization" of aliens, 113
Anderson, P. J., 134
Andersonian Institute, 54
Andover Theological Seminary. *See* Harvard University, Andover Theological Seminary
Anglican Church, 8, 42, 84
Anglo-American cataloguing code, 69, 119
Anglo-Saxon manuscripts, 13
Anne, Queen, 17, 27, 137
Ansell, E., 148
Apprentices' libraries, 91-2, 151
Arabic literature, 7
Arabic manuscripts, 9
Archaeological literature, 100
Architectural literature, 7
Architecture, library. *See* Library buildings and names of specific libraries
Aretino, Pietro, 7
Aristotelianism, 23
Armstrong College Library, 62, 144
Army Medical Library. *See* Surgeon General's Library
Art, literature of, 7, 117
Arts End, 73
Arts Libraries, University of London, 47
Arundel, Earl of. *See* Howard, Thomas
Arundel House, 15
Arundel manuscripts, 33

Index

Ascham, Roger, 12
Ashburnham House, 29
Asher (bookdealer), 36
Ashley, F. W., 158
Ashmole, Elias, 23
Association of College and Reference Libraries. *See* American Library Association, College and Reference Section
Association of Special Libraries and Information Bureaux, 62, 144, 147
Association of University Teachers (England), 71
Astor, John Jacob, 109
Astor, Lenox, and Tilden Foundations, 110, 155
  See also Lenox Library and New York Public Library
Astor Library, 94, 106, 110
  See also New York Public Library
Astronomical literature, 16
Athenaeum, 40, 69, 144
Athenaeum Club, 61
Auctions, 12, 20, 26, 33, 36, 51
Axon, W. E. A., 139, 142
Ayer Collection, 106

Baber, Henry, 35, 38, 39
Bacon, Francis, 14, 16, 24, 67, 145
Bacon, Nicholas, 14
Bacteriological literature, 101
Bagford, John, 134
Baker, E. A., 132, 143
Baker Memorial Library. *See* Dartmouth College Library building
Balcarres, Earls of, 15, 51
  library. *See* Biblioteca Lindesiana
Bale, John, 13, 133
Ballinger, 143
Baltimore, 110
  Enoch Pratt Free Library, 105, 109
    building, 123, 124
Bancroft, Richard, 9, 14, 135
Bandinel, Bulkeley, 25
Banks, Joseph, 32, 38, 68, 138
Barlow, Thomas, 19
Barnard, Frederick, 32
Barnett, C. R., 158
Barocci Collection, 9
Barrow, Isaac, 24
Barwick, G. F., 144
Batman, Stephen, 22, 136
Baum, Wilhelm, 101, 153
Bay Psalm Book, 150
Beatty, R. C., 150

Bechstein, R., 100, 153
Beckford, William, 51, 141
Belden, C. F. D., 155
Bell, Andrew, 53
Bennett, H. L., 134
Bensly, Edward, 137
Bentham, Jeremy, 47, 55, 67, 145
Bentley, Richard, 13, 24, 27, 28, 134, 136, 138
Berelson, B. R., 159
Berkeley, George, 25
Berkeley, William, 149
Bernays, J., 100, 153
Bible, New Testament, 100, 124
Bibliographical Society of America, 156
Biblioteca Lindesiana, 15, 51
Biblioteca Spenceriana. *See* Althorp Library
Bickley, A. C., 135
Billings, John Shaw, 108, 152, 157
Birkbeck, George, 54, 136, 142
Birmingham (England), 71, 143
  Public Library, 57, 59, 144
Bishop, William Warner, 104, 112, 116, 152, 153, 154, 155, 156, 157
Blenheim Library. *See* Marlborough, Dukes of, library
Bliss, H. E., 158
Bluntschli, J. K., 101
Board of Education. *See* Great Britain, Board of Education
Boase, G. C., 142
Bodleian Library, 8, 9, 10, 14, 15, 18, 19, 20, 21, 25-6, 27, 38, 43-4, 45, 64, 65, 66, 67, 71, 72, 73-4, 85, 135, 136, 137, 140, 145
  building, 73-4, 75, 140, 143, 148
  catalogue, 20-1, 26, 31, 137, 146
  commissions of investigation. *See* Great Britain, Commission on the State, Discipline, Studies, and Revenues of the University and Colleges of Oxford and Oxford University, Commission Appointed by the Congregation of the University
  See also Old Library, Oxford, Oxford Publick Library, and Humphrey, Duke of Gloucester, library
Bodley, Thomas, 6, 8, 11, 13, 16, 17, 18, 19, 26, 135, 136
  autobiography, 133
  family, 135
Bogeng, Gustav Adolf Erich, 134, 136, 141, 155

Index

College of Physicians Library, Phila-
delphia, 97
Colonial Institute Library, 61
Colonial libraries (American), 53, 84-8
Columbia University, 150, 154
  library, 103, 125, 154
    building, 123, 124
  School of Library Economy, 125
  School of Library Service, 127, 158
Compleat Gentleman, 12
Consultantships. *See* Library of Congress
  consultantships
Cooke, A. S., 147
Coolidge, A. C., 101
Coolidge, Elizabeth Sprague. *See* Elizabeth
  Sprague Coolidge Gift
Cooper, C. H., 133, 135, 137
Cooper, Thompson, 136
Cooperation, library, 60, 62, 70-2, 117, 120,
  144, 147
Coptic manuscripts, 36
Copyright, 8, 12, 22, 25, 27-8, 66, 96, 116,
  137, 145
  See also License Acts
Cornell University, 99
  Library, 103, 153
Cornwall, 71
Corpus Christi College Library, Cam-
  bridge, 14, 17, 27
Correspondence courses, 112
Cotton family, 138
  See also Great Britain, Parliament,
    House of Commons, Committee on
    the Cottonian Library
Cotton, John, 16
Cotton, Robert, 6, 14, 15, 16, 17, 19, 22
Cotton, Thomas, 16
Cotton House, 16
Cotton Library, 29
County libraries (American), 95, 109, 111-
  12, 155
  California, 111
County libraries (England), 70-1, 147
Courtney, W. P., 139
Coutts, James, 134
Cowell, Peter, 144
Cowley, J. D., 146
Cowtan, Robert, 137
Craftsman, 25
Cranmer, Thomas, 12, 13
Craster, H. H. E., 148
Crawford, Earls of, 51
  Library. *See* Biblioteca Lindesiana
Credland, W. R., 143

Crerar, John, 109
  See also John Crerar Library
Cromwell, Oliver, 11, 19
Cromwell, Thomas, 5, 7
Cuaderno de ortografía, 151
Cudworth, Ralph, 24
Curriculum. *See* Library schools, curricu-
  lum
Curtius, Ernst, 153
Curzon, George N., 140, 145
Cuthbertson, David, 134
Cutter, Charles Ammi, 51, 68, 69, 107, 118,
  125, 141, 156, 157, 158
  Expansive Classification devised by, 120

Dana, John Cotton, 105, 106, 107, 154
Danton, J. Perriam, 158
Dartmouth College, 150
  Library, 85
    building, 123
Davis, W. L., 141, 148
Deane, Charles, 149
Decimal Classification. *See* Brussels Classi-
  fication and Dewey, Melvil, Decimal
  Classification devised by
Dee, John, 6, 16, 22
Delivery stations, 109
Dell, William, 23
Democrats, 89
Departmental libraries (in universities), 47,
  75, 154
  See also Seminar libraries
Departmental organization, 57, 62, 75, 105,
  122-3
Deposit collections, 57, 110
Depository legislation (government docu-
  ments), 96
  See also Copyright and License Acts
Depression, 113
Deutsche Gesellschaft in Pennsylvanien,
  150
Devereux, Robert, 14
Dewey, Melvil, 107, 112, 118, 119, 125, 126,
  128, 149, 158, 159
  Decimal Classification devised by, 120,
    168
Dibdin, Thomas Frognall, 32, 51, 138, 141
Dibelius, Wilhelm, 141, 144
Dickson, W. K., 141
Dickson, W. P., 134, 136
Digby, Kenelm, 9, 133
Dilke, Charles, 69
Discussion groups, 113
Doctorate, 99

Index

Index

177

The American Library Association, established in 1876, is an organization of libraries, librarians, library trustees and others interested in the responsibilities of libraries in the educational, social and cultural needs of society. It is affiliated with more than fifty other library associations in this country and abroad. It works closely with many organizations concerned with education, recreation, research, and public service. Its activities are carried on by a headquarters staff, voluntary boards and committees, and by divisions, sections, and round tables, all interested in various aspects or types of library service. Its program includes information and advisory services, personnel service, field work, annual and midwinter conferences, and the publication—not for profit—of numerous professional books, pamphlets and periodicals.

Date Due